THE WORD AS
ARCHIPELAGO

THE WORD AS ARCHIPELAGO

René Char

TRANSLATED BY ROBERT BAKER

OMNIDAWN PUBLISHING
RICHMOND, CALIFORNIA
2012

Cover art: Lascaux Cave, frieze of swimming stags.
(Photo N. Aujoulat-CNP-MCC.)

Book cover and interior design by Cassandra Smith

Omnidawn Publishing is committed to preserving ancient forests and natural resources. We elected to print this title on 30% postconsumer recycled paper, processed chlorine-free. As a result, for this printing, we have saved:

5 Trees (40' tall and 6-8" diameter)
2,238 Gallons of Wastewater
2 million BTUs of Total Energy
142 Pounds of Solid Waste
496 Pounds of Greenhouse Gases

Omnidawn Publishing made this paper choice because our printer, Thomson-Shore, Inc., is a member of Green Press Initiative, a nonprofit program dedicated to supporting authors, publishers, and suppliers in their efforts to reduce their use of fiber obtained from endangered forests.

For more information, visit www.greenpressinitiative.org

Environmental impact estimates were made using the Environmental Defense Paper Calculator. For more information visit: www.edf.org/papercalculator

Library of Congress Cataloging-in-Publication Data

Char, René, 1907-1988.
[Parole en archipel. English]
The word as archipelago / René Char ; translated by Robert Baker.
p. cm.
Includes bibliographical references.
ISBN 978-1-890650-47-6 (pbk. : alk. paper)
I. Baker, Robert, 1965- II. Title.
PQ2605.H3345P313 2012
841'.912--dc23
                    2012014454

Published by Omnidawn Publishing, Richmond, California
www.omnidawn.com   (510) 237-5472   (800) 792-4957
10 9 8 7 6 5 4 3 2 1
ISBN 978-1-890650-47-6

CONTENTS

POÈMES DES DEUX ANNÉES / POEMS OF TWO YEARS

LA BIBLIOTHÈQUE EST EN FEU ET AUTRES POÈMES / THE LIBRARY IS
ON FIRE AND OTHER POEMS

QUITTER / DEPARTING

RENÉ CHAR

THE HERMETIC BOUNDARY BETWEEN
THE SHADOW AND THE LIGHT

Fury and Mystery

Fureur et mystère, fury and mystery, is the title of a major postwar collection
gathering the work Char wrote between 1938 and 1948. It could serve as a
title for his work as a whole. Mystery refers to the spaces of poetry: the earth
and sky, the horizon of vision, an almost apparitional depth in what comes
to be. Fury refers to our longing for the fuller life the mystery promises. In
"Mission and Revocation," a sort of epilogue to the long sequence *Partage
formel* (Formal Share), Char, looking in wonder at the things around him,
poses a question: "Forms endowed with life, extraordinary things, plain
things, I ask: 'Inner Command? Summons from without?'" (*Œuvres*, 169).
Though the question is not given a direct answer, the suggestion is, clearly,
both at once. The summons from without is the mystery. The inner command
is the fury.

Char has many names and figures for the mystery that poetry brings to
light in words. Sometimes he calls it the open, or the summit, or the upland,
or the unknown. At times he figures it as the transparence of dawn, akin to the
divine dawn that Rimbaud pursues in one of the simplest of his *Illuminations*.
Elsewhere he imagines it as the clarity of a night within the night, beyond the
night, akin to the "cool transparent night" that Whitman is drawn to. Often,
in a tradition at least as old as Plato's *Symposium*, he calls it Beauty. Frequently
he conceives it as an ascent, an immanent transcendence that holds to the
things of earth and the burdens of history. Throughout his work this ascent is
linked to *l'Amie*, the Beloved, the call of love. In his later work, in particular,
it tends to be associated with a meditative space. According to his biographer,
Char said that he felt this presence and promise from his earliest years on. "She
was not in me, but near me. Even as a child, I truly felt there was someone
holding herself at my side, invisible, and who was not God. . . . And my life

has unfolded with the desire for this presence, so ephemeral and so powerful" (Greilsamer, 26). Summons from without.

The desire for this presence is a dimension of what Char means by fury. *Fureur* simply means rage or fury, but it also has valences like those of the Latin *furor* and the old Italian *furore*, and on this level it suggests passion, vehemence, enthusiasm, transport. Char's *fureur* indeed has affinities with Blake's Orc: a general force of sexual desire, social rebellion, and existential longing. A defiance animates his work as it animated his life. He quit high school, his last year, in sheer exasperation. For five years in his twenties he participated in the manifold rebellion of the surrealist movement. Between 1940 and 1944, during the occupation and division of France, he joined the Resistance and became an effective leader. He always retained a decisive independence of mind. Such defiance, as he saw it, was an ally of the life of eros and the élan of poetry. To love freedom was to love all that mattered. "I only find my being, I only want to live, in the space and freedom of my love" ("Lettera Amorosa," 31). Char belongs to a roving tradition that runs from Shelley through Paul Éluard and Miguel Hernández, among many others, and even his poems that are not love poems are in the end love poems. He is in love with life, *la vie inexprimable*, inexpressible life, as he calls it in a poem from the thirties (*Œuvres*, 81). Eros goes toward a space of genuine encounter. Char variously speaks of this eros as love, passion, generosity, stubbornness, exuberance, enthusiasm. "Long body that felt the demanding enthusiasm, / Now perpendicular to the wounded Beast," he says of the dead bird-man, perhaps a shaman, in the famous painting at Lascaux (43). The passionate hunter has been undone in his pursuit of the mystery. There's no end to the undoing. Recovery is always necessary. The bird-man is also a "dancer in the abyss, spirit, ever to be born," in a movement of renewal. Inner command.

Trajectory

Char was born in 1907, in L'Isle-sur-la-Sorgue, a small village in the Vaucluse that, as the name suggests, is located on the Sorgue River. His father, a well-to-do businessman, died when he was ten. He and his three siblings—two older sisters and a bullying older brother—were raised by his mother and at times by his grandmother. He was always an individual who set his own course. After leaving the lycée in his last year, he enrolled in a business school in Marseille for a year, devoting his time not to the study of business but to the reading and writing of poetry. In the fall of 1929, he sent an early book to Éluard, an already recognized poet nearly twelve years his senior, who befriended him. By November of that year Char was in Paris and a member of the surrealist movement. He would remain a participant until 1935, and his work from the late twenties and early thirties, collected in *Le Marteau sans maître* (The Hammer without a Master), shows the signs of this initiation: a provocative irreverence, a fascination with dream, a dispersive exuberance. Yet in the mid-thirties Char distanced himself from surrealism.

In the second half of the thirties, in solitude in Provence, he undertook a reorientation, seeking a poetry that would provide a "productive knowledge of the real" (*Œuvres*, 63). At the time he experienced a severe illness that led to a brush with death. The late thirties were of course years of ominous signs on every side: the Popular Front government in France was falling apart; the Spanish Republic was being destroyed; the fascist "hypnosis" or "monster," as Char called it, was descending on Europe. Char's last major publications of this period, which appeared in 1937 and 1938, were *Placard pour un chemin des écoliers* (A Poster for the Long Path of Schoolchildren), a book dedicated to the children of Spain; *Dehors la nuit est gouvernée* (Outside the Night Is Governed); and *Le Visage nuptial* (Nuptial Face). He served in the French army, in Alsace, from September 1939 through June 1940, when the routed and demoralized French surrendered. He then returned home, to a south of France under the Vichy regime, and in 1941, seeking to escape police surveillance (his surrealist activities had made him suspect), departed for Céreste, a small mountain village. There he made contact with other dissidents and helped form a Resistance network that was in place by 1942. In 1943–44 he became a commander in the Secret Army, *capitaine Alexandre*, in charge of the Lower Alps region. By all accounts he was a clear-eyed and inspiring leader. The Allies invaded France in the summer of 1944, and in late August the nation was liberated.

Throughout the war Char published nothing, choosing what his biographer calls a principled silence, and yet, amid all his other responsibilities, he found time to write a great deal. Among the works he wrote in these years are a series of prose poems at once lyrical and political, *Seuls demeurent* (They Alone Remain); a metapoetic sequence of metaphysical range, *Partage formel*

(Formal Share); and a wartime notebook—practical, grounded, fierce, lyrical, humanist—titled *Feuillets d'Hypnos* (Leaves of Hypnos). The last of these, published in 1946, would be considered one of the great works of testimony to come out of the French Resistance. All of these writings, many other poems of the period, the earlier *Visage nuptial,* and a sequence of poems written shortly after the war, *Le Poème pulvérisé* (The Pulverized Poem), were gathered in the major collection *Fureur et mystère* published in 1948. Char's furious hope, tried in severe circumstances, had survived intact. It would animate the distinctive alliances of his mature work: vehemence and poise, conciseness and spaciousness, lyrical circumference and philosophical clarity.

To some extent Char's defiant energy of the forties seems to have carried him through the fifties. But there were, of course, darker consequences to what he had endured, which brought periods of severe depression and persistent insomnia. There were, too, his vexations with the postwar political and cultural climate, though he was hardly isolated, having in these years renewed his friendship with Éluard, formed a close friendship with several well-known painters and writers, including Georges Braque and Albert Camus, and become the generous mentor of some of the inventive younger poets of the decade, notably André du Bouchet and Jacques Dupin. Char's immediate impulse after the war, it seems, was to return to the sustaining sources of his art in lyrical encounter, in sweeping retrievals of older layers of experience in the rural world of his youth, as is seen with particular resonance in the poems of creative memory collected in *Le Poème pulvérisé.* This impulse was important throughout the postwar period. Under thoroughly different circumstances, then, the fifties were as productive a time of writing for Char as the catastrophic forties had been. Several major works were written in this decade: *Les Matinaux* (which might be translated as "those who rise to meet the dawn" or "the dawn breakers"); *À une sérénité crispée* (To a Tense Serenity); *Lettera Amorosa* (later included as the first poem of The Word as Archipelago); *Recherche de la base et du sommet* (Search for the Base and the Summit), a volume of essays on painters and writers important to Char as well as concise accounts of his years in the Resistance; and *La Parole en archipel* (The Word as Archipelago), a book published in 1962 but collecting poems from the previous decade. Char's work of the sixties through the eighties, from *Retour amont* (Returning Upland) through the late *Éloge d'une soupçonnée* (In Praise of an Intuited Presence), extended further a certain meditative turn. Voyage through the spaces of "unadorned night" has an ample place in the later work. Char died in 1988. The last poem of his last book is a love poem.

The interplay of fury and mystery animates the whole of Char's trajectory. The poles of this tension receive different emphases, measure each other in different ways, during different phases of the journey. And while there is no simple linear path, it is true that fury tends to predominate in the early poems, those of his passage through the surrealist movement, while a crossing toward the mystery, whether visionary or meditative, tends to predominate in the later poems. Perhaps the period of Char's work that is often thought to be the greatest in force and range—that of the forties and fifties—most fully holds together both sides of this alliance. *The Word as Archipelago* includes many of his major poems of the fifties. There are poems that recall the experience of the war years; love poems and poems of friendship; poems that explore writing, awakened perception, intent recovery; poems of quest and encounter; poems of departure in the night. In this sense *The Word as Archipelago* is at once a gathering and a presage of another phase of the journey. And the title of the book speaks as suggestively of the form of Char's poetry as the title *Fury and Mystery* speaks of the basic poles of its substance.

The Word as Archipelago

"Poetry is at once word and the silent desperate provocation that we are, demanding the coming of a reality without rival," Char writes in "During the Journey" (187), the outer summons here being imagined as a coming reality, the inner command as a desperate passion. Poetry, for Char, is at once this space of crossing forces and the constellated word that makes this space audible and nearly visible. If fury and mystery are dimensions of the life of encounter, they are also dimensions of a formal practice.

Char moves with ease among different forms: metrical verse, free verse, the prose poem, and the aphoristic sequence, as well as the highly concentrated essay that tilts toward the prose poem. But it is fair to say that the prose poem and the aphoristic sequence lend a distinctive formal signature to his work. These two forms readily turn into one another. The aphoristic sequences, even when largely consisting of aphorisms of one or two sentences, often include a slightly longer aphorism that approaches a brief prose poem. The prose poems are sometimes extremely concise, formed of two or three sentences, as in the section of this book titled "Above the Wind," which one might read as an aphoristic sequence or as a series of highly compressed prose poems. Other poems here, like "The Room in Space" or "The Ascent of Night," seem to hover on a boundary between long-legged free verse and the aphoristic sequence. "My métier, at the cutting edge, is a métier of point," Char says in "The Library Is on Fire" (111), and it is clear that the carved, evocative, speculative phrase, surrounded by silence, is a fundamental element of his art. He is inclined toward what George Oppen— in a very different sort of work—calls a "poetry of statement," or, one might say, of multiple and contradictory statements on a path. He is in search of bearings to live by. His words are sharp and open, worked to a shine and left en route.

Every reader will arrive at his or her own way of inhabiting this movement, of seeing what experience looks and feels like on this route. In "We Have," the first poem of the last section of this book, Char writes: "Our word as archipelago gives you, after grief and disaster, strawberries it brings from the moors of death, and fingers warm from having gathered them" (183). The expression "the word as archipelago" suggests a dialectic of the concrete and the distant, the visible and the invisible. It nearly sounds like a surmise about the space of surmise. Figures that rhyme with this figure appear throughout Char's work: the pulverized poem; a path that is a shattered walking stick; a presence that flies into pieces as one approaches it; a springtime scattered across the seasons; a startling apparition that a startled individual tries to translate into a galaxy; a long sentence of the sky of which our words, spoken as we walk along a road, are fragments; the formal share or dividing out that one writer composes of a larger gift that is in itself inexpressible. The gift, like the wolf chased in "Muttering," is there and yet far. One might think of an archipelago in air. Perhaps all of Char's parables and aphorisms are like the hills, folds, and peaks of a mountain range that speaks of weight and ascent, earth and horizon. "The urgent, jagged, bold writing of a blue lantern—of Ventoux in its childhood—always ran on the horizon of Montmirail that at every moment our love brought me, took away from me" (197). According to Jean-Claude Mathieu, Char once said that the landscapes of Provence were themselves aphoristic.

In Char's work, as in any writer's work, many precursors are refracted. Rimbaud would seem to be the most important influence on his writing, present in the compressed prose poem, in the quickness of articulation, in the alternation between abrupt departure and hymnal embrace, in the visionary search embedded in the realm of natural presence (Lawler, 95), in the habit of psychic voyage. Char, it could be said, tempers and deepens Rimbaud, drawing his desperate energy into the space of love and the poise of meditative reach. Perhaps it could be said, too, that Char tempers and deepens the surrealist faith in revelatory encounter and the incongruous image. His verse poems, if sometimes steep or angular, are sometimes of a light or popular mode that has a long French tradition behind it. It is especially intriguing to consider what sources might have led Char to the sort of aphoristic sequences he wrote from the thirties through the eighties. There are several possible sources: the classical French moralists, Nietzsche, a range of romantic writers at times given to an aphoristic mode, from Schlegel and Novalis to Blake and again Rimbaud. Perhaps there is an echo of the wisdom literature of various ancient traditions. There is surely a link with the elliptical practices of certain currents in modernist writing. Char himself liked to emphasize a connection with Heraclitus (at least in the fragmentary form in which the latter's work has come down to us). The philosopher of time, fire, the interpenetration of opposites, the thinking in images: this is one of Char's adopted sources.

In 1948 Char wrote a brief preface to a French translation of Heraclitus (*Œuvres*, 720–21). It is, as Paul Veyne has said, a quite Nietzschean essay. Many others, including Camus, have found in Char a "Heraclitean" vision of life. Char reads Heraclitus as a philosopher of tragic pessimism and large-spirited affirmation despite all. Everything is ruin and astonishment, sheer transience and sheer disclosure. In all his work Char embraces the movement of parallels, tensions, or oppositions: fury and mystery, pessimism and hope, point and amplitude, perceptual ardor and meditative patience, the poet's unfolded premonition and the Maquis's practical resistance. "At the center of poetry," he writes in *À une sérénité crispée*, "there awaits one who contradicts you. He is your sovereign. Wrestle loyally with him" (*Œuvres*, 754).

For Char, as for Nietzsche, as for Camus, we dwell in contradiction, in the dark and the light, on the border of the known and the unknown, threatened by the ten thousand fetters of despair, called by the ten thousand dimensions of wonder. The question is how to live in this "rebellious and solitary world of contradictions" (*Œuvres*, 247). Perhaps we are given a hint in "The Black Stags," the second poem of Char's "Lascaux" sequence, which tells of stags that have "swept across millennial space / From the rock's darkness to the air's caresses" (43). The stags invoked in the poem, probably those known to scholars of the Lascaux caves as "the swimming stags," seem in the original painting to be crossing a river, though this could be simply an accident of the rock, or an accident of the rock that an ancient painter has brought into vision. The stags are crossing a river of accident, fortune, becoming. They are rising from an invisibility of sixteen thousand years to a visibility in the present. They are ascending from rock to air, from hiddenness to disclosure. Pursued by a hunter, bodied forth as image by a painter, invoked by the poet of this poem, they appear "on the hermetic boundary between the shadow and the light," as Char puts it in "During the Journey." "We can only live in the half-opened, exactly on the hermetic boundary between the shadow and the light. But we are irresistibly thrown ahead. Our whole being lends support and vertigo to this push" (187). This is an essential concern in Char's poetry. Elsewhere he writes: "We must build and dwell outside ourselves, on the edge of tears and in the orbit of famines, if we wish for something uncommon to take place, solely for us" (183).

What would this uncommon disclosure be? We could guess that it would involve defiance, freedom, love, deepened vision. Char's *Feuillets d'Hypnos* includes twenty-five or thirty concise portraits of individuals with whom he lived and worked in the Resistance. One of these portraits consists of a few words said by Roger Chaudon, a generous man who was killed by the Gestapo a month before the liberation. Char admired him greatly. Near the end of *Feuillets d'Hypnos* he writes: "A few days before his execution, Roger Chaudon said to me: 'On this earth, one is occasionally up, for the most part down. The order of these periods cannot be altered. It is this, at bottom, that brings me calm, despite the joy in life that shakes me like thunder'" (*Œuvres*, 231). This portrait of Chaudon is perhaps an indirect portrait of Char as well. This is the "tragic optimism" that Camus found in Char. It is the "goodness of despair, unconditional, independent of every scientific or metaphysical justification" that Georges Mounin found in Char (167). It is the Nietzschean pessimism and affirmation, the *amor fati*, that Veyne found in Char. It is the tragic sense and noble spirit that Char found in Heraclitus. Dominique Fourcade, in words spoken shortly after Char's death, said that not only Char's poetry but also his conversation transfigured the everyday, that in his presence "everything became fire" (cited in Greilsamer, 459–60). Char is the poet of an affirmation that shakes one like thunder. In his eyes, this has to be found again and again, amid all that that destroys it again and again, outside ourselves and within ourselves. The swimming stags, crossing a river of time in perfect quiet, are an image of enthusiasm.

Translation

A translator is inevitably concerned with a boundary of a certain sort: a boundary between two languages. Char has been widely translated in other countries. At least until recently, he has been translated less fully here in the United States. Over the years there have been important editions of selected poems, from the work of Jackson Mathews in the fifties, *Hypnos Waking*, to the edition of Mary Ann Caws and Tina Jolas in the early nineties, *Selected Poems*, to the book published a few years ago by Nancy Naomi Carlson, *Stone Lyre*. There have been translations of some of his individual works, too, though not as many as one would wish for. Impressive accomplishments in this realm include both Jackson Mathews's and Cid Corman's translations of *Leaves of Hypnos*, Gustaf Sobin's translations of *The Brittle Age* and *Returning Upland*, and Mary Ann Caws and Nancy Kline's recent translation of the major work *Furor and Mystery* (in a volume including selected poems from other works). Michael Worton's translation of *The Dawn Breakers* was published in England twenty years ago. My translation of *The Word as Archipelago* is meant to bring this book as a whole into the field of Char's work available in English.

There is always the question of what is or isn't brought over in a translation. It is sometimes said that there are as many versions of a poet as there are translations, just as there are as many versions of a poet as there are readers, and this is true in a sense that every reader of poetry understands. There is nevertheless a standard for reading set by what is shown in the work encountered: by what is felt, seen, thought, said in the work.

Any translation of Char, I think, will be judged by its ability to bring into English at least three defining qualities of his work. The first is a conjunction of vivid concreteness and speculative scope: a conjunction true to the half-opened, to the hermetic boundary between the shadow and the light. The second is a voice that, while of course various, responsive to different occasions and intentions, has nonetheless a predominant tone: a tone, to borrow language from Char himself, of "serene vehemence," of "tense serenity." It's a voice that tells of the thirst and the water at once (*Œuvres*, 608). A third quality runs through every element of Char's work. I would characterize it as an incisiveness that is at once a quickness, a compression, and an expansiveness. This is palpable, first of all, at the level of the word as archipelago. But this level is itself a formal figure, a written analogue of a way of inhabiting being, as Maurice Merleau-Ponty would say, an expressive disclosure of a way of inhabiting a life. This is among the most important gifts that a poet—at least a poet in Char's tradition—gives to a reader.

These brief comments, of course, are not meant to provide a comprehensive account of what is impressive in Char's work. I mean only to make explicit the standards I've felt to be especially significant in translating this work. A translator, having taken the journey, can only leave the poems for the encounter of each reader. "Truth is personal," Char says on more than one occasion, in the voice of an existentialist, for it is found on the particular path of a particular life and all its commitments. And yet this singular perspective opens onto a widened community of illumination. As Char puts it in *Rougeur des Matinaux* (Redness of the *Matinaux*): "The personal adventure, the miraculous adventure, community of our dawns."

Bibliography

Char's Poetry

The Brittle Age and *Returning Upland*. Translated by Gustaf Sobin, with a foreword by Mary Ann Caws. Denver: Counterpath Press, 2009.

The Dawn Breakers. Translated and with an inroduction by Michael Worton. Newcastle upon Tyne: Bloodaxe Books, 1992.

Furor and Mystery. Translated by Mary Ann Caws and Nancy Kline, with an introduction by Sandra Bermann and a foreword by Marie-Claude Char. Boston: Black Widow Press, 2010.

Hypnos Waking. Edited by Jackson Mathews; translated by Jackson Mathews and others. New York: Random House, 1956.

Leaves of Hypnos. Translated by Cid Corman. New York: Grossman Publishers, 1973.

Œuvres complètes. Revised edition. Edited and with an introduction, chronology, and notes by Jean Roudaut. Paris: Gallimard, 1995.

Poems of René Char. Translated by Mary Ann Caws and Jonathan Griffin. Princeton: Princeton University Press, 1976.

Selected Poems. Edited by Mary Ann Caws and Tina Jolas; translated by Mary Ann Caws and others, with an introduction by Caws. New York: New Directions, 1992.

Stone Lyre: Poems of René Char. Translated by Nancy Naomi Carlson, with an introduction by Ilya Kaminsky. North Adams, MA: Tupelo Press, 2009.

This Smoke That Carried Us: Selected Poems. Translated by Susanne Dubroff, with an introduction by Christopher Merrill. Buffalo: White Pine Press, 2004.

CRITICISM

Baker, Robert. *In Dark Again in Wonder: The Poetry of René Char and George Oppen*. Notre Dame: The University of Notre Dame Press, 2012.

Blanchot, Maurice. "René Char." In *The Work of Fire*, translated by Charlotte Mandell, 98–110. Stanford: Stanford University Press, 1995.

———. "René Char and the Thought of the Neutral." In *The Infinite Conversation*, translated and with a foreword by Susan Hanson, 298–306. Minneapolis: University of Minnesota Press, 1993.

Bosch, Elizabeth. "René Char, Georges Bataille, et Lascaux." In *Lectures de René Char*, ed. Tineke Kingma-Eijgendaal and Paul J. Smith, 98–117. Amsterdam: Rodopi, 1990.

Camus, Albert. "René Char." In *Lyrical and Critical Essays*, ed. Philip Thody and trans. Ellen Conroy Kennedy, 321–25. New York: Knopf, 1968.

Caws, Mary Ann. *The Presence of René Char*. Princeton: Princeton University Press, 1976.

Fourcade, Dominique. "Essai d'introduction." In *René Char*, ed. Fourcade. Special edition of *L'Herne* 15 (1971): 19–30.

Greilsamer, Laurent. *L'Éclair au front: La vie de René Char*. Paris: Fayard, 2004.

La Charité, Virginia. *The Poetics and the Poetry of René Char*. Chapel Hill: University of North Carolina Press, 1968.

Lawler, James. *René Char: The Myth and the Poem*. Princeton: Princeton University Press, 1978.

Marty, Eric. *René Char*. Paris: Seuil, 1990.

Mathieu, Jean-Claude. *La Poésie de René Char*. 2 vols. Paris: José Corti, 1988, 1990.

Mounin, Georges. *La Communication poétique*. Paris: Gallimard, 1969.

Piore, Nancy Kline. *Lightning: The Poetry of René Char*. Boston: Northeastern University Press, 1981.

Poulet, Georges. "René Char." In *Le Point de départ*, 92–108. Paris: Plon, 1964.

Richard, Jean-Pierre. "René Char." In *Onze études sur la poésie moderne*, 81–127. Paris: Seuil, 1964.

Velay, Serge. *René Char*. Lyon: La Manufacture, 1987.

Veyne, Paul. *René Char en ses poèmes*. Paris: Gallimard, 1990.

LETTERA AMOROSA

LETTERA AMOROSA

LETTERA AMOROSA

Non è già part'in voi che con forz' invincibile
d'amore tutt' a se non mi tragga.

Monteverdi, *Lettera amorosa*

Temps en sous-œuvre, années d'affliction . . . Droit naturel! Ils donneront malgré eux une nouvelle fois l'existence à l'Ouvrage de tous les temps admiré.

Je te chéris. Tôt dépourvu serait l'ambitieux qui resterait incroyant en la femme, tel le frelon aux prises avec son habileté de moins en moins spacieuse. Je te chéris cependant que dérive la lourde pinasse de la mort.

«Ce fut, monde béni, tel mois d'Éros altéré, qu'elle illumina le bâti de mon être, la conque de son ventre: je les mêlai à jamais. Et ce fut à telle seconde de mon appréhension qu'elle changea le sentier flou et aberrant de mon destin en un chemin de parélie pour la félicité furtive de la terre des amants.»

LETTERA AMOROSA

> *Non è già part'in voi che con forz' invincibile*
> *d'amore tutt' a se non mi tragga.*
>
> Monteverdi, *Lettera amorosa*

Time restored from within, years of affliction . . . By nature! They will, despite themselves, again give life to the Work admired in all times.

I adore you. Soon at a loss would be the ambitious man who lacked a faith in woman, like a hornet locked in a fight with his own cleverness, becoming less and less spacious. I adore you while the heavy pinnace of death drifts.

"It was, blessed world, in a month of Eros thirsting that she illumined the structure of my being, the shell of her womb: I merged them forever. It was in a moment of my disquiet that she changed the blurred, aberrant trail of my destiny into a path of luminous rings for the secret joy of the lovers' earth."

*Le cœur soudain privé, l'hôte du désert devient
presque lisiblement le cœur fortuné, le cœur agrandi,
le diadème.*

. . . Je n'ai plus de fièvre ce matin. Ma tête est de nouveau claire et vacante,
posée comme un rocher sur un verger à ton image. Le vent qui soufflait du
Nord hier, fait tressaillir par endroits le flanc meurtri des arbres.

Je sens que ce pays te doit une émotivité moins défiante et des yeux autres
que ceux à travers lesquels il considérait toutes choses auparavant. Tu es partie
mais tu demeures dans l'inflexion des circonstances, puisque lui et moi avons
mal. Pour te rassurer dans ma pensée, j'ai rompu avec les visiteurs éventuels,
avec les besognes et la contradiction. Je me repose comme tu assures que je
dois le faire. Je vais souvent à la montagne dormir. C'est alors qu'avec l'aide
d'une nature à présent favorable, je m'évade des échardes enfoncées dans ma
chair, vieux accidents, âpres tournois.

Pourras-tu accepter contre toi un homme si haletant?

Lunes et nuit, vous êtes un loup de velours noir, village, sur la veillée de
mon amour.

«Scrute tes paupières», me disait ma mère, penchée sur mon avant-
sommeil d'écolier. J'apercevais flottant un petit caillou, tantôt paresseux,
tantôt strident, un galet pour verdir dans l'herbe. Je pleurais. Je l'eusse voulu
dans mon âme, et seulement là.

Chant d'Insomnie:

*Amour hélant, l'Amoureuse viendra,
Gloria de l'été, ô fruits!
La flèche du soleil traversera ses lèvres,
Le trèfle nu sur sa chair bouclera,
Miniature semblable à l'iris, l'orchidée,
Cadeau le plus ancien des prairies au plaisir
Que la cascade instille, que la bouche délivre.*

The heart suddenly bereft, the host of the desert becomes, almost legibly, the heart made fortunate, the widened heart, the diadem.

. . . I have no more fever this morning. My head is again clear and vacant, posed like a rock above an orchard formed in your image. Here and there, the wind that blew yesterday from the North makes the battered sides of the trees tremble.

I feel this countryside owes you a less combative susceptibility, and eyes other than those through which it has previously seen things. You have departed, yet you remain in the inflection of circumstances, for the countryside and myself are aching. To calm you in my thought, I have broken with potential visitors, with labors and contradiction. I rest as you tell me I should. Often I go to the mountain to sleep. It's then that, with the help of a nature now become promising, I escape the thorns stuck in my flesh, old accidents, bitter contests.

Could you accept beside you a man so desperately breathing?

Moons and night, you are a wolf of black velvet, a village, over the vigil of my love.

"Examine your eyelids," my mother would say, bending over my fore-sleep at the end of a day of school. I saw a little stone floating, now idle, now abrupt, a pebble to grow green in the grass. I wept. I would have liked it in my soul, and there alone.

Song of Insomnia

With the cry of Love, the Lover will come,
The Gloria of summer, oh fruits!
The arrow of the sun will pierce her lips,
The naked clover on her flesh will bend,
A miniature like the iris, the orchid,
The prairies' most ancient gift to the pleasure
The waterfall brings, the mouth relieves.

Je voudrais me glisser dans une forêt où les plantes se refermeraient et s'étreindraient derrière nous, forêt nombre de fois centenaire, mais elle reste à semer. C'est un chagrin d'avoir, dans sa courte vie, passé à côté du feu avec des mains de pêcheur d'éponges. «Deux étincelles, tes aïeules», raille l'alto du temps, sans compassion.

Mon éloge tournoie sur les boucles de ton front, comme un épervier à bec droit.

L'automne! Le parc compte ses arbres bien distincts. Celui-ci est roux traditionnellement; cet autre, fermant le chemin, est une bouillie d'épines. Le rouge-gorge est arrivé, le gentil luthier des campagnes. Les gouttes de son chant s'égrènent sur le carreau de la fenêtre. Dans l'herbe de la pelouse grelottent de magiques assassinats d'insectes. Écoute, mais n'entends pas.

Parfois j'imagine qu'il serait bon de se noyer à la surface d'un étang où nulle barque ne s'aventurerait. Ensuite, ressusciter dans le courant d'un vrai torrent où tes couleurs bouillonneraient.

Il faut que craque ce qui enserre cette ville où tu te trouves retenue. Vent, vent, vent autour des troncs et sur les chaumes.

J'ai levé les yeux sur la fenêtre de ta chambre. As-tu tout emporté? Ce n'est qu'un flocon qui fond sur ma paupière. Laide saison où l'on croit regretter, où l'on projette, alors qu'on s'aveulit.

L'air que je sens toujours prêt à manquer à la plupart des êtres, s'il te traverse, a une profusion et des loisirs étincelants.

Je ris merveilleusement avec toi. Voilà la chance unique.

Absent partout où l'on fête un absent.

Je ne puis être et ne veux vivre que dans l'espace et dans la liberté de mon amour. Nous ne sommes pas ensemble le produit d'une capitulation, ni le motif d'une servitude plus déprimante encore. Aussi menons-nous malicieusement l'un contre l'autre une guérilla sans reproche.

I would like to slip into a forest where the plants closed and held each other behind us, a forest centuries old, though still to be sown. It's a sorrow, in a brief life, to have passed beside the fire with the hands of a fisher of sponges. "Two sparks, your ancestors," the alto of time scoffs, without pity.

My praise circles like a hard-beaked hawk above the locks on your brow.

Autumn! The park counts its various trees. This one is traditionally red; that one, blocking the path, is a welter of thorns. The robin has arrived, the gentle luthier of the fields. The drops of his song ripple on the windowpane. Enchanted assassinations of insects shiver on the lawn. Listen without quite hearing.

Sometimes I imagine that it would be well to drown in the shallow water of a pond where no boat would venture. Then to be revived in the current of an authentic torrent foaming with your colors.

All that encloses the city where you're being held must be broken. Wind, wind, wind around the trees and above the stubble fields.

I've raised my eyes to the window of your room. Have you carried everything away? It's only a snowflake that melts on my eyelid. Ugly season where one thinks one regrets, where one plans, where in fact one grows weaker.

The air I perceive as always about to die around most beings, in sweeping over you, pours forth and sparkles with leisure.

I laugh marvelously with you. There's the singular luck.

Absent wherever we celebrate someone absent.

I only find my being, I only want to live, in the space and freedom of my love. Together we are hardly the product of a capitulation, or the intent of some still more depressing servitude. We mischievously carry out against each other a guerilla war beyond reproach.

Tu es plaisir, avec chaque vague séparée de ses suivantes. Enfin toutes à la fois chargent. C'est la mer qui se fonde, qui s'invente. Tu es plaisir, corail de spasmes.

Qui n'a pas rêvé, en flânant sur le boulevard des villes, d'un monde qui, au lieu de commencer avec la parole, débuterait avec les intentions?

Nos paroles sont lentes à nous parvenir, comme si elles contenaient, séparées, une sève suffisante pour rester closes tout un hiver; ou mieux, comme si, à chaque extrémité de la silencieuse distance, se mettant en joue, il leur était interdit de s'élancer et de se joindre. Notre voix court de l'un à l'autre; mais chaque avenue, chaque treille, chaque fourré, la tire à lui, la retient, l'interroge. Tout est prétexte à la ralentir.
Souvent je ne parle que pour toi, afin que la terre m'oublie.

Après le vent c'était toujours plus beau, bien que la douleur de la nature continuât.

Je viens de rentrer. J'ai longtemps marché. Tu es la Continuelle. Je fais du feu. Je m'assois dans le fauteuil de panacée. Dans les plis des flammes barbares, ma fatigue escalade à son tour. Métamorphose bienveillante alternant avec la funeste.

Dehors le jour indolore se traîne, que les verges des saules renoncent à fustiger. Plus haut, il y a la mesure de la futaie que l'aboi des chiens et le cri des chasseurs déchirent.

Notre arche à tous, la très parfaite, naufrage à l'instant de son pavois. Dans ses débris et sa poussière, l'homme à tête de nouveau-né réapparaît. Déjà mi-liquide, mi-fleur.

La terre feule, les nuits de pariade. Un complot de branches mortes n'y pourrait tenir.

S'il n'y avait sur terre que nous, mon amour, nous serions sans complices et sans alliés. Avant-coureurs candides ou survivants hébétés.

You are pleasure, with each wave separated from those that follow. Finally they all charge at once. It's the sea that founds itself, invents itself. You are pleasure, coral that quivers.

Who, strolling along city boulevards, hasn't dreamed of a world that, instead of beginning with the word, would dawn with intentions?

Our words are slow to come to us, as if they contained, each of them, enough sap to hold themselves in store an entire winter; or as if, at both ends of a silent distance, while taking aim, they were kept from leaping and joining one another. Our voice runs from one to the other; but each avenue, each arbor, each thicket draws it to itself, holds it, questions it. Everything is an occasion to slow it down.

Often I speak only for you, so that the earth will forget me.

The weather was always more beautiful after the wind, however much the suffering of nature continued.

I've just returned. I walked a long time. You are the Continual. I make a fire. I sit in the healing chair. In the folds of the savage flames, my fatigue ascends in turn. Benevolent metamorphosis in alternation with the fatal one.

Outside the insipid day drags itself along; the willow branches have given up flaying it. Higher up, there's a forest rent by the howling of dogs and the cries of hunters.

Our ark for everyone, perfected, founders the moment it sets to sea. Amid its debris and dust, the man with the head of a newborn reappears. Already half-liquid, half-flower.

The earth growls on nights when birds mate. No conspiracy of dead branches could endure it.

If there were no one on earth but us, my love, we would be without accomplices and without allies. Candid forerunners or dazed survivors.

L'exercice de la vie, quelques combats au dénouement sans solution mais aux motifs valides, m'ont appris à regarder la personne humaine sous l'angle du ciel dont le bleu d'orage lui est le plus favorable.

Toute la bouche et la faim de quelque chose de meilleur que la lumière (de plus échancré et de plus agrippant) se déchaînent.

Celui qui veille au sommet du plaisir est l'égal du soleil comme de la nuit. Celui qui veille n'a pas d'ailes, il ne poursuit pas.

J'entrouvre la porte de notre chambre. Y dorment nos jeux. Placés par ta main même. Blasons durcis, ce matin, comme du miel de cerisier.

Mon exil est enclos dans la grêle. Mon exil monte à sa tour de patience. Pourquoi le ciel se voûte-t-il?

Il est des parcelles de lieux où l'âme rare subitement exulte. Alentour ce n'est qu'espace indifférent. Du sol glacé elle s'élève, déploie tel un chant sa fourrure, pour protéger ce qui la bouleverse, l'ôter de la vue du froid.

Pourquoi le champ de la blessure est-il de tous le plus prospère? Les hommes aux vieux regards, qui ont eu un ordre du ciel transpercé, en reçoivent sans s'étonner la nouvelle.

Affileur de mon mal je souffre d'entendre les fontaines de ta route se partager la pomme des orages.

Une clochette tinte sur la pente des mousses où tu t'assoupissais, mon ange du détour. Le sol de graviers nains était l'envers humide du long ciel, les arbres des danseurs intrépides.

Trêve, sur la barrière, de ton museau repu d'écumes, jument de mauvais songe, ta course est depuis longtemps terminée.

Cet hivernage de la pensée occupée d'un seul être que l'absence s'efforce de placer à mi-longueur du factice et du surnaturel.

The practice of life, some struggles that ended without solution but whose motives were valid, have taught me to look at the human individual under the angle of the storm-blue sky most favorable to him.

The whole mouth and the hunger of something better than the light (more jagged and more gripping) are set loose.

He who stays awake at the summit of pleasure is the equal of both sun and night. He who stays awake has no wings, is done with pursuit.

I crack open the door of our room. Our games are sleeping there. Put there by your very hand. Hardened emblems, this morning, like the honey of the cherry tree.

My exile is held fast in the hail. My exile climbs to its tower of patience. Why does the sky bend down?

There are places, fragments of places, where the uncommon soul suddenly rejoices. The surrounding area is indifferent space. The soul rises from the frozen ground, extends her coat like a song to protect that which has stunned her, to take it from the sight of the cold.

Why is the field of the wound the most flourishing of all? Men with old eyes, bearers of an order from the pierced sky, receive such news without alarm.

A sharpener of my own pain, I suffer from hearing the fountains of your path sharing the storms' apple.

A small bell rings on the moss-covered slope where you were dozing, my angel of detour. The gravelly soil was the moist back of the long sky, the trees intrepid dancers.

Enough of your frothing muzzle at the fence, mare of bad dreams, your race ended long ago.

This wintering through of thought preoccupied with a single being, which absence tries to place halfway between the invented and the supernatural.

Ce n'est pas simple de rester hissé sur la vague du courage quand on suit du regard quelque oiseau volant au déclin du jour.

Je ne confonds pas la solitude avec la lyre du désert. Le nuage cette nuit qui cerne ton oreille n'est pas de neige endormante, mais d'embruns enlevés au printemps.

Il y a deux iris jaunes dans l'eau verte de la Sorgue. Si le courant les emportait, c'est qu'ils seraient décapités.

Ma convoitise comique, mon vœu glacé: saisir ta tête comme un rapace à flanc d'abîme. Je t'avais, maintes fois, tenue sous la pluie des falaises, comme un faucon encapuchonné.

Voici encore les marches du monde concret, la perspective obscure où gesticulent des silhouettes d'hommes dans les rapines et la discorde. Quelques-unes, compensantes, règlent le feu de la moisson, s'accordent avec les nuages.

Merci d'être, sans jamais te casser, iris, ma fleur de gravité. Tu élèves au bord des eaux des affections miraculeuses, tu ne pèses pas sur les mourants que tu veilles, tu éteins des plaies sur lesquelles le temps n'a pas d'action, tu ne conduis pas à une maison consternante, tu permets que toutes les fenêtres reflétées ne fassent qu'un seul visage de passion, tu accompagnes le retour du jour sur les vertes avenues libres.

It's not easy to stay hoist on a wave of courage while one's eyes follow a bird flying at the end of day.

I don't confuse solitude with the lyre of the desert. The cloud that embraces your ear tonight is not tedious snow but spindrift taken from the spring.

There are two yellow irises in the green water of the Sorgue. If the current were to carry them off, one would say they had been decapitated.

My comic lust, my cold vow: to seize your head like a hawk at the edge of the abyss. Many times I've held you, like a hooded falcon, under the rain of the cliffs.

Here, again, the affairs of the practical world, the darkened dimension where silhouettes of men flail about in plundering and discord. A few, to compensate, take care of the harvest fire, align themselves with the clouds.

All my thanks, iris, for being my flower of gravity that never breaks. You raise miraculous affections on the waters' shores, you do not weigh upon the dying you keep watch over, you close wounds that time has no effect on, you lead to no dismaying house, you permit all reflected windows to form a single face of passion, you accompany the day's return to quickened avenues of freedom.

SUR LE FRANC-BORD

I. IRIS.   1. Nom d'une divinité de la mythologie grecque, qui était la messagère des dieux. Déployant son écharpe, elle produisait l'arc-en-ciel.
2. Nom propre de femme, dont les poètes se servent pour désigner une femme aimée et même quelque dame lorsqu'on veut taire le nom.
3. Petite planète.

II. IRIS. Nom spécifique d'un papillon, le nymphale gris, dit le grand mars changeant. Prévient du visiteur funèbre.

III. IRIS. Les yeux bleus, les yeux noirs, les yeux verts, sont ceux dont l'iris est bleu, est noir, est vert.

IV. IRIS. Plante. Iris jaune des rivières.

. . . Iris plural, iris d'Éros, iris de *Lettera amorosa*.

ON THE FREEBOARD

I. IRIS. 1. Name of a divinity in Greek mythology, a messenger of the gods. Unfurling her scarf, she produced the rainbow.

2. Proper name of a woman, used by poets to designate a loved woman, or a lady, when they wish to conceal her true name.

3. Small planet.

II. IRIS. Particular name of a butterfly, the gray nymphalid, known as the "great changing Mars." Signals the approach of a funereal visitor.

III. IRIS. Blue eyes, black eyes, green eyes: eyes of which the iris is blue, black, green.

IV. IRIS. Plant. Yellow iris of the rivers.

. . . Plural iris, iris of Eros, iris of *Lettera amorosa*.

LA PAROI ET LA PRAIRIE

THE ROCK WALL AND THE MEADOW

LASCAUX

I

HOMME-OISEAU MORT ET BISON MOURANT

Long corps qui eut l'enthousiasme exigeant,
À présent perpendiculaire à la Brute blessée.

Ô tué sans entrailles!
Tué par celle qui fut tout et, réconciliée, se meurt;
Lui, danseur d'abîme, esprit, toujours à naître,
Oiseau et fruit pervers des magies cruellement sauvé.

II

LES CERFS NOIRS

Les eaux parlaient à l'oreille du ciel.
Cerfs, vous avez franchi l'espace millénaire,
Des ténèbres du roc aux caresses de l'air.

Le chasseur qui vous pousse, le génie qui vous voit,
Que j'aime leur passion, de mon large rivage!
Et si j'avais leurs yeux, dans l'instant où j'espère?

LASCAUX

I

DEAD BIRD-MAN AND DYING BISON

Long body that felt the demanding enthusiasm,
Now perpendicular to the wounded Beast.

O slain without a wound!
Slain by she who was everything and, reconciled, dies;
He, dancer in the abyss, spirit, ever to be born,
Magic's bird and unhallowed fruit cruelly saved.

II

THE BLACK STAGS

The waters were speaking into the ear of the sky.
Stags, you have swept across millennial space,
From the rock's darkness to the air's caresses.

The hunter who chases you, the genius who sees you,
How I love their passion, from my ample shore!
And if I had their eyes, in the moment when I hope?

III

LA BÊTE INNOMMABLE

La Bête innommable ferme la marche du gracieux troupeau, comme un
    cyclope bouffe.
Huit quolibets font sa parure, divisent sa folie.
La Bête rote dévotement dans l'air rustique.
Ses flancs bourrés et tombants sont douloureux, vont se vider de leur
    grossesse.
De son sabot à ses vaines défenses, elle est enveloppée de fétidité.

Ainsi m'apparaît dans la frise de Lascaux, mère fantastiquement déguisée,
La Sagesse aux yeux pleins de larmes.

IV

JEUNE CHEVAL À LA CRINIÈRE VAPOREUSE

Que tu es beau, printemps, cheval,
Criblant le ciel de ta crinière,
Couvrant d'écume les roseaux!
Tout l'amour tient dans ton poitrail:
De la Dame blanche d'Afrique
À la Madeleine au miroir
L'idole qui combat, la grâce qui médite.

III

THE UNNAMABLE BEAST

The unnamable Beast brings up the rear of the graceful herd, like a vulgar
    cyclops.
Eight gibes form her finery, divide up her madness.
The Beast solemnly belches in the country air.
Her stuffed, hanging belly is aching, is about to be emptied of its child.
From her hoof to her futile tusks, she is enveloped in filth.

Thus appears to me in the painting at Lascaux, strange disguised mother,
Wisdom with her eyes full of tears.

IV

YOUNG HORSE WITH A MANE OF VAPOR

Ah you are beautiful, springtime, horse,
Riddling the sky with your mane,
Covering the reeds in foam!
All of love would fit in your chest:
From the white Lady of Africa
To the Magdalen beside the mirror,
The god that fights, the grace that meditates.

TRANSIR

Cette part jamais fixée, en nous sommeillante, d'où jaillira DEMAIN LE MULTIPLE.

L'âge du renne, c'est-à-dire l'âge du souffle. Ô vitre, ô givre, nature conquise, dedans fleurie, dehors détruite!

Insouciants, nous exaltons et contrecarrons justement la nature et les hommes. Cependant, terreur, au-dessus de notre tête, le soleil entre dans le signe de ses ennemis.

La lutte contre la cruauté profane, hélas, vœu de fourmi ailée. Sera-t-elle notre novation?

Au soleil d'hiver quelques fagots noués et ma flamme au mur.

Terre où je m'endors, espace où je m'éveille, qui viendra quand vous ne serez plus là? (*que deviendrai-je* m'est d'une chaleur presque infinie).

CHILLING

This never stable element, dormant in us, from which will spring forth
TOMORROW THE MULTIPLE.

The age of the reindeer, that is to say, the age of the breath. O windowpane,
O frost, nature conquered, flowering within, destroyed without!

Insouciant, we justly rouse and vie with nature and others. Nevertheless,
terror, above our heads the sun is entering the sign of its enemies.

The struggle against profane cruelty, alas, vow of the winged ant. Will it
be our novation?

Under the winter sun a few bundles of sticks and my flame at the wall.

Earth where I fall asleep, space where I awake, who will come when you
are no longer there? (*what will I become* bears for me an almost infinite heat).

QUATRE FASCINANTS

I

LE TAUREAU

Il ne fait jamais nuit quand tu meurs,
Cerné de ténèbres qui crient,
Soleil aux deux pointes semblables.

Fauve d'amour, vérité dans l'épée,
Couple qui se poignarde unique parmi tous.

II

LA TRUITE

Rives qui croulez en parure
Afin d'emplir tout le miroir,
Gravier où balbutie la barque
Que le courant presse et retrousse,
Herbe, herbe toujours étirée,
Herbe, herbe jamais en répit,
Que devient votre créature
Dans les orages transparents
Où son cœur la précipita?

FOUR THAT FASCINATE

I

THE BULL

It's never night when you die,
Surrounded by the dark that cries,
Sun with two parallel points.

Love's wildness, truth in the sword,
Incomparable couple that rends itself.

II

THE TROUT

Shores that collapse brilliantly
In order to fill the entire mirror,
River stones where the boat stammers
That the current hurries and rolls,
Grass, grass always unfolded,
Grass, grass never at rest,
What is it your creature becomes
In the transparent storms
Its heart hurled it into?

III

LE SERPENT

Prince des contresens, exerce mon amour
À tourner son Seigneur que je hais de n'avoir
Que trouble répression ou fastueux espoir.

Revanche à tes couleurs, débonnaire serpent,
Sous le couvert du bois, et en toute maison.
Par le lien qui unit la lumière à la peur,
Tu fais semblant de fuir, ô serpent marginal!

IV

L'ALOUETTE

Extrême braise du ciel et première ardeur du jour,
Elle reste sertie dans l'aurore et chante la terre agitée,
Carillon maître de son haleine et libre de sa route.

Fascinante, on la tue en l'émerveillant.

III

THE SERPENT

Prince of mistakes, give practice to my love
In slipping past her Lord, the one I hate
For having but dull repression, luxurious hope.

Revenge of your colors, genial serpent,
Under cover of the woods and in every house.
Through the tie that links the light to fear,
You pretend to flee, O serpent of the margins!

IV

THE LARK

Pure ember of the sky and first ardor of the day,
She is set in the dawn like a jewel and sings the shaken earth,
Soaring chime who's master of her breath and free in her route.

Ah she fascinates: one pierces her by astonishing her.

LA MINUTIEUSE

L'inondation s'agrandissait. La campagne rase, les talus, les menus arbres désunis s'enfermaient dans des flaques dont quelques-unes en se joignant devenaient lac. Une alouette au ciel trop gris chantait. Des bulles çà et là brisaient la surface des eaux, à moins que ce ne fût quelque minuscule rongeur ou serpent s'échappant à la nage. La route encore restait intacte. Les abords d'un village se montraient. Résolus et heureux nous avancions. Dans notre errance il faisait beau. Je marchais entre Toi et cette Autre qui était Toi. Dans chacune de mes mains je tenais serré votre sein nu. Des villageois sur le pas de leur porte ou occupés à quelque besogne de planche nous saluaient avec faveur. Mes doigts leur cachaient votre merveille. En eussent-ils été choqués? L'une de vous s'arrêta pour causer et pour sourire. Nous continuâmes. J'avais désormais la nature à ma droite et devant moi la route. Un bœuf au loin, en son milieu, nous précédait. La lyre de ses cornes, il me parut, tremblait. Je t'aimais. Mais je reprochais à celle qui était demeurée en chemin, parmi les habitants des maisons, de se montrer trop familière. Certes, elle ne pouvait figurer parmi nous que ton enfance attardée. Je me rendis à l'évidence. Au village la retiendraient l'école et cette façon qu'ont les communautés aguerries de temporiser avec le danger. Même celui d'inondation. Maintenant nous avions atteint l'orée de très vieux arbres et la solitude des souvenirs. Je voulus m'enquérir de ton nom éternel et chéri que mon âme avait oublié: «Je suis la Minutieuse.» La beauté des eaux profondes nous endormit.

LA MINUTIEUSE

The flood was widening. The bare fields, the embankments, the slender dispersed trees were disappearing in pools, some of which came together to form a lake. A lark sang in the too gray sky. Bubbles here and there broke the surface of the water, unless these were tiny rodents or serpents that could escape by swimming. The road was still intact. The outskirts of a village appeared. Resolved and happy, we went forward. In our wandering the weather was beautiful. I walked between You and that Other who was You. In my hands I held close your naked breasts. Villagers on their doorsteps or occupied with chores greeted us kindly. My fingers hid your marvel from them. Would they have been shocked? One of you stopped to chat and smile. We continued. Thereafter I had nature on my right and the road before me. An ox in the distance, in a space of its own, preceded us. It seemed that the lyre of its horns trembled. I loved you. But I reproached the one who had remained behind, among the house dwellers, for having shown herself too familiar. It was clear that for us she could represent only your lingering childhood. I ceded to the evidence. They would keep her in the village, through education and the way hardened communities have of temporizing with danger, even the danger of a flood. Now we had reached the edge of the oldest trees and the solitude of memories. I asked about your eternal and cherished name that my soul had forgotten. "I am *la Minutieuse*." The beauty of the deep waters lulled us to sleep.

POÈMES DES DEUX ANNÉES

POEMS OF TWO YEARS

I

LE REMPART DE BRINDILLES

I

THE RAMPART OF TWIGS

VERS L'ARBRE-FRÈRE AUX JOURS COMPTÉS

Harpe brève des mélèzes,
Sur l'éperon de mousse et de dalles en germe
—Façade des forêts où casse le nuage—,
Contrepoint du vide auquel je crois.

TO BROTHER TREE WHOSE DAYS ARE NUMBERED

Brief harp of larches,
On the spur of moss and emergent rocks
—Façade of forests where the cloud breaks—
Counterpoint of the void in which I believe.

LE REMPART DE BRINDILLES

Le dessein de la poésie étant de nous rendre souverains en nous impersonnalisant, nous touchons, grâce au poème, à la plénitude de ce qui n'était qu'esquissé ou déformé par les vantardises de l'individu.

Les poèmes sont des bouts d'existence incorruptibles que nous lançons à la gueule répugnante de la mort, mais assez haut pour que, ricochant sur elle, ils tombent dans le monde nominateur de l'unité.

Nous sommes déroutés et sans rêve. Mais il y a toujours une bougie qui danse dans notre main. Ainsi l'ombre où nous entrons est notre sommeil futur sans cesse raccourci.

Lorsque nous sommes aptes à monter à l'aide de l'échelle naturelle vers quelque sommet initiant, nous laissons en bas les échelons du bas; mais quand nous redescendons, nous faisons glisser avec nous tous les échelons du sommet. Nous enfouissons ce pinacle dans notre fonds le plus rare et le mieux défendu, au-dessous de l'échelon dernier, mais avec plus d'acquisitions et de richesses encore que notre aventure n'en avait rapporté de l'extrémité de la tremblante échelle.

Ne cherche pas les limites de la mer. Tu les détiens. Elles te sont offertes au même instant que ta vie évaporée. Le sentiment, comme tu sais, est enfant de la matière; il est son regard admirablement nuancé.

Jeunes hommes, préférez la rosée des femmes, leur cruauté lunatique, à laquelle votre violence et votre amour pourront riposter, à l'encre inanimée des meurtriers de plume. Tenez-vous plutôt, rapides poissons musclés, dans la cascade.

Nous vivons collés à la poitrine d'une horloge qui, désemparée, regarde finir et commencer la course du soleil. Mais elle courbera le temps, liera la terre à nous; et cela est notre succès.

Si la tempête en permanence brûle mes côtes, mon onde au large est profonde, complexe, prestigieuse. Je n'attends rien de *fini*, j'accepte de godiller entre deux dimensions inégales. Pourtant mes repères sont de plomb, non de liège, ma trace est de sel, non de fumée.

THE RAMPART OF TWIGS

The purpose of poetry being to make us sovereign by impersonalizing us, we touch, thanks to the poem, the fullness of that which was only suggested or deformed by the boastings of the individual.

Poems are those pieces of incorruptible existence that we hurl at the repugnant maw of death, hurl sufficiently high that, ricocheting back, they fall into the world where names for the whole are found.

We are disoriented and without a dream. But there is always a candle that dances in our hand. Thus the shadow we enter is our future sleep continually cut short.

When we are able, with the help of the ladder of nature, to climb toward some initiatory summit, we leave below the lower rungs; yet when we return, we bring with us all the rungs of the summit. We bury the pinnacle in the rarest and best defended of our depths, beneath the last rung, where there are still more finds and riches than our adventure had brought back from the highest point of the trembling ladder.

Do not seek the boundaries of the sea. You possess them. They are given to you at the same moment as your vanishing life. Feeling, you know, is the child of matter, its marvelously subtle eye.

Young men, prefer the dew of women, their capricious cruelty, to which your violence and your love can respond, to the lifeless ink of those who kill with a pen. Hold yourselves like quick, vigorous fish in the cascade.

We live attached to the breast of a clock that, unprotected, watches the sun's journey end and begin. But it will bend time, connect the earth to us; and that is our accomplishment.

If the perpetual storm burns my coasts, my wave at sea is deep, complex, prestigious. I don't expect anything *finished*, I embrace a sculling between two unequal dimensions. Yet the markers of my passage are of lead, not cork, my wake is of salt, not smoke.

Échapper à la honteuse contrainte du choix entre l'obéissance et la démence, esquiver l'abat de la hache sans cesse revenante du despote contre laquelle nous sommes sans moyens de protection, quoique étant aux prises sans trêve, voilà notre rôle, notre destination, et notre dandinement justifiés. Il nous faut franchir la clôture du pire, faire la course périlleuse, encore chasser au delà, tailler en pièces l'inique, enfin disparaître sans trop de pacotilles sur soi. Un faible remerciement donné ou entendu, rien d'autre.

Combien s'imaginent porter la terre et exprimer le monde, qui trépignent de ne pouvoir s'informer mielleusement de leur destin auprès de la Pythie.

Je crois en Lui: il n'est pas.
Je ne m'en rapporte pas à lui: est-Il?
Principe de tout avancement, de tout dégagement. Nuit ouverte et glacée! Ah! fin de la chaîne des démentis.
(La quête d'un grand Être, n'est-ce qu'une pression de doigt du présent entravé sur l'avenir en liberté? Les lendemains non touchés sont vastes. Et là-bas est divin où ne retentit pas le choc de notre chaîne.)

Êtres que l'aurore semble laver de leurs tourments, semble doter d'une santé, d'une innocence neuves, et qui se fracassent ou se suppriment deux heures après . . . Êtres chers dont je sens la main.

La cheminée du palais de même que l'âtre de la chaumière fument depuis que la tête du roi se trouve sur les chenets, depuis que les semelles du représentant du peuple se chauffent naïvement à cette bûche excessive qui ne peut pas se consumer malgré son peu de cervelle et l'effroi de ceux pour lesquelles elle fut guillotinée. Entre les illusions qui nous gouvernent, peut-être reverra-t-on celles, dans l'ordre naturel appelées, que quelque aspect du sacré tempère et qui sont au regard averti les moins cyniquement dissimulées. Mais cette apparition, que les exemples précédents ont disqualifiée, doit attendre encore, car elle est sans énergie et sans bonté dans des limbes que le poison mouille. La propriété redevenant l'infini impersonnel à l'extérieur de l'homme, la cupidité ne sera plus qu'une fièvre d'étape que chaque lendemain absorbera. Tout l'embasement néanmoins est à réinventer. La vie bousillée est à ressaisir, avec tout le doré du couchant et la promesse de l'éveil, successivement. Et honneur à la mélancolie augmentée par l'été d'un seul jour, à midi impétueux, à la mort.

To escape the humiliating constraint of a choice between obedience and insanity, to dodge the stroke of the despot's ever returning axe, against which we are without protection though ceaselessly battling, this is our role, our purpose, and our awkwardly swaying gait. We must leap the fence of the worst, trace a perilous course, hunt yet further beyond, cut the iniquitous in pieces, at last disappear without much show. A faint thanks given or heard, nothing more.

How many imagine they carry the earth and voice the world but only stamp their feet, their sugary requests of the Pythia having earned them no knowledge of their destiny.

I believe in Him: he is not.
I do not rely on him: is He?
Principle of all advance, all release. Open and frozen night! Ah! end of the chain of refutations.
(The quest for a superior Being, is it not simply a push of the finger of the shackled present upon the future that's free? The untouched tomorrows are vast. And the place where our chain no longer rattles is divine.)

Beings that dawn seems to wash of their torments, to endow with a new health and innocence, and that are shattered or destroyed two hours later . . . Lovely beings whose hands I sense.

Both the palace fireplace and the cottage hearth are smoking since the king's head was found on the andirons, since the feet of the people's representative naively sought warmth by this blazing log that does not die out, despite its dimness of mind and the fear of those for whom it was guillotined. Among the illusions that govern us, perhaps we will see a return of those, summoned in the natural course of things, which some aspect of the sacred tempers and which to the experienced eye are the least cynically disguised. But this apparition, disqualified by the examples just given, will have to wait, for in the poison-drenched limbo it is without energy and goodness. When property again becomes the impersonal infinite exterior to man, avarice will be only a passing fever that every tomorrow absorbs. The whole foundation is nevertheless to be reinvented. Botched life is to be seized again, with all the gold of sunset and all the promise of awakening, successively. And honor to the melancholy deepened by the summer of a single day, at impetuous noon, honor to death.

Tour à tour coteau luxuriant, roc désolé, léger abri, tel est l'homme, le bel homme déconcertant.

Disparu, l'élégance de l'ombre lui succède. L'énigme a fini de rougir.

Nota. — Cessons de miroiter. Toute la question sera, un moment, de savoir si la mort met bien le point final à tout. Mais peut-être notre cœur n'est-il formé que de la réponse qui n'est point donnée?

Et la faculté de fine manœuvre? Qui sera ton lecteur? Quelqu'un que ta spéculation arme mais que ta plume innocente. Cet oisif, sur ses coudes? Ce criminel encore sans objet? Prends garde, quand tu peux, aux mots que tu écris, malgré leur ferme distance.

By turns abundant hillside, desolate rock, lightened shelter, such is man, beautiful and disconcerting man.

When he disappears, the elegance of the shadow succeeds him. The enigma has finished blushing.

Nota. — Enough of this drama. The whole question, at a certain moment, will be to know if death indeed puts an end to everything. But perhaps our heart is formed only of the response not given?

And the power of deft maneuver? Who will be your reader? Someone that your speculation arms but that your pen absolves. This idler on his elbows? This criminal still without a plan? If possible, watch out for the words you write, however clearly marked their distance.

L'INOFFENSIF

Je pleure quand le soleil se couche parce qu'il te dérobe à ma vue et parce que je ne sais pas m'accorder avec ses rivaux nocturnes. Bien qu'il soit au bas et maintenant sans fièvre, impossible d'aller contre son déclin, de suspendre son effeuillaison, d'arracher quelque envie encore à sa lueur moribonde. Son départ te fond dans son obscurité comme le limon du lit se délaye dans l'eau du torrent par-delà l'éboulis des berges détruites. Dureté et mollesse au ressort différent ont alors des effets semblables. Je cesse de recevoir l'hymne de ta parole; soudain tu n'apparais plus entière à mon côté; ce n'est pas le fuseau nerveux de ton poignet que tient ma main mais la branche creuse d'un quelconque arbre mort et déjà débité. On ne met plus un nom à rien, qu'au frisson. Il fait nuit. Les artifices qui s'allument me trouvent aveugle.

Je n'ai pleuré en vérité qu'une seule fois. Le soleil en disparaissant avait coupé ton visage. Ta tête avait roulé dans la fosse du ciel et je ne croyais plus au lendemain.

Lequel est l'homme du matin et lequel celui des ténèbres?

THE HARMLESS INDIVIDUAL

I weep when the sun goes down because it steals you from my sight and I don't know how to reconcile myself with its nocturnal rivals. Even if the sun is now low in the sky and without fever, it's impossible to resist its decline, suspend its unleafing, wrest some last longing from its dying glimmer. Its departure melts you in darkness as the silt of the river is thinned in the torrent beyond the loose rock of its destroyed banks. Hardness and softness, if having different motives, then have similar effects. I cease to receive the hymn of your word; suddenly you no longer appear whole at my side; it's not the nervous spindle of your wrist that my hand holds but the empty branch of a dead tree already cut into pieces. One no longer gives a name to anything, except to the shivering. It's dark. Even the fireworks they set off find me blind.

In truth I have wept only a single time. The sun in disappearing had severed your face. Your head had rolled into the grave of the sky and I no longer believed in tomorrow.

Which is the man of morning, and which the man of darkness?

LE MORTEL PARTENAIRE

Il la défiait, s'avançait vers son cœur, comme un boxeur ourlé, ailé et puissant, bien au centre de la géométrie attaquante et défensive de ses jambes. Il pesait du regard les qualités de l'adversaire qui se contentait de rompre, cantonné entre une virginité agréable et son expérience. Sur la blanche surface où se tenait le combat, tous deux oubliaient les spectateurs inexorables. Dans l'air de juin voltigeait le prénom des fleurs du premier jour de l'été. Enfin une légère grimace courut sur la joue du second et une raie rose s'y dessina. La riposte jaillit sèche et conséquente. Les jarrets soudain comme du linge étendu, l'homme flotta et tituba. Mais les poings en face ne poursuivirent pas leur avantage, renoncèrent à conclure. À présent les têtes meurtries des deux battants dodelinaient l'une contre l'autre. À cet instant le premier dut à dessein prononcer à l'oreille du second des paroles si parfaitement offensantes, ou appropriées, ou énigmatiques, que de celui-ci fila, prompte, totale, précise, une foudre qui coucha net l'incompréhensible combattant.

Certains êtres ont une signification qui nous manque. Qui sont-ils? Leur secret tient au plus profond du secret même de la vie. Ils s'en approchent. Elle les tue. Mais l'avenir qu'ils ont ainsi éveillé d'un murmure, les devinant, les crée. Ô dédale de l'extrême amour!

THE FATAL PARTNER

All defiance, he advanced toward life's heart, like a threatened boxer, winged and powerful in the center of his legs' aggressive and defensive geometry. As he weighed with his eyes the skills of the adversary, the latter was content with breaking off, well stationed between an attractive virginity and a store of experience. On the white canvas where the fight was held, both forgot the inexorable spectators. There fluttered in the June air the first names of the flowers of the first day of summer. At last a faint grimace crossed the adversary's face, a red scratch appeared. The riposte shot forth clean and emphatic. The first, his knees suddenly like sheets hung out to dry, floated and staggered. But the fists that had struck him chose not to pursue their advantage, refused to conclude. Now the bruised heads of the two fighters nodded against each other. At this moment the first must have deliberately whispered in the ear of the second words so perfectly offensive, or appropriate, or enigmatic, that the second delivered a lightning blow—swift, absolute, precise—that laid the incomprehensible fighter out cold.

Certain beings have a meaning that eludes us. Who are they? Their secret comes from the deepest secret of life itself. They approach. Life kills them. But the future they have thus awakened with a murmur, in guessing them, creates them. O labyrinth of sheer love!

FRONT DE LA ROSE

Malgré la fenêtre ouverte dans la chambre au long congé, l'arôme de la rose reste lié au souffle qui fut là. Nous sommes une fois encore sans expérience antérieure, nouveaux venus, épris. La rose! Le champ de ses allées éventerait même la hardiesse de la mort. Nulle grille qui s'oppose. Le désir resurgit, mal de nos fronts évaporés.

Celui qui marche sur la terre des pluies n'a rien à redouter de l'épine, dans les lieux finis ou hostiles. Mais s'il s'arrête et se recueille, malheur à lui! Blessé au vif, il vole en cendres, archer repris par la beauté.

THE ROSE'S BROW

The window is open in the long-abandoned room, and yet the rose's fragrance remains bound to the breath that was once there. Again we are without experience, newly arrived, captivated, in love. The rose! Its spacious paths would cool even death's audacity. No gate's in the way. Desire looms again, ache in our lightened brow.

He who walks the earth of rains has nothing to fear from the thorn, in spent or hostile places. But if he stops to gather his thoughts, woe to him! Wounded to the quick, he flies apart in ashes, archer recaptured by beauty.

II

L'AMIE QUI NE RESTAIT PAS

II

THE BELOVED WHO DID NOT STAY

LA DOUBLE TRESSE

CHAUME DES VOSGES

Beauté, ma toute-droite, par des routes si ladres,
À l'étape des lampes et du courage clos,
Que je me glace et que tu sois ma femme de décembre.
Ma vie future, c'est ton visage quand tu dors.

1939

SUR LA PAUME DE DABO

Va mon baiser, quitte le frêle gîte,
Ton amour est trouvé, un bouleau te le tend.
La résine d'été et la neige d'hiver
Ont pris garde.

Été 1953

THE DOUBLE BRAID

The Stubble of Vosges

Beauty, my entirely upright, along the barren roads,
In this hour of lamps and sealed courage,
May I be ice and you my December woman.
My future life is your face when you're asleep.

1939

In Dabo's Palm

Go, my kiss, abandon the frail shelter,
Your love is found, a birch tree offers it to you.
Summer's resin and winter's snow
Have taken it in mind.

Summer 1953

FIÈVRE DE LA PETITE-PIERRE D'ALSACE

Nous avancions sur l'étendue embrasée des forêts, comme l'étrave face aux lames, onde remontée des nuits, maintenant livrée à la solidarité de l'éclatement et de la destruction. Derrière cette cloison sauvage, au delà de ce plafond, retraite d'un stentor réduit au silence et à la ferveur, se trouvait-il un ciel?

Nous le vîmes à l'instant que le village nous apparut, bâtisse d'aurore et de soir nonchalant, nef à l'ancre dans l'attente de notre montée.

Bonds obstinés, marche prospère, nous sommes à la fois les passants et la grand-voile de la mer journalière aux prises avec des lignes, à l'infini, de barques. Tu nous l'apprends, sous-bois. Sitôt le feu mortel traversé.

FEVER OF LA PETITE-PIERRE D'ALSACE

We were advancing across the blazing expanse of forests, like the keel fronting the waves, depth of nights rising again, now abandoned to the solidarity of explosion and destruction. Behind this wall of wild growth, beyond this ceiling, refuge of a loud voice reduced to fervor and silence, was there a sky to be found?

We saw it the moment the village appeared, structure of dawn and nonchalant evening, ship at anchor awaiting our boarding.

Untiring leaps, lively pace, we are at once passersby and the mainsail of the daily sea fighting endless rows of skiffs. You teach it to us, forest undergrowth. As soon as the mortal fire is passed through.

LA PASSE DE LYON

Je viendrai par le pont le plus distant de Bellecour, afin de vous laisser le loisir d'arriver la première. Vous me conduirez à la fenêtre où vos yeux voyagent, d'où vos faveurs plongent quand votre liberté échange sa lumière avec celle des météores, la vôtre demeurant et la leur se perdant. Avec mes songes, avec ma guerre, avec mon baiser, sous le mûrier ressuscité, dans le répit des filatures, je m'efforcerai d'isoler votre conquête d'un savoir antérieur, autre que le mien. Que l'avenir vous entraîne avec des convoiteurs différents, j'y céderai, mais pour le seul chef-d'œuvre!

Flamme à l'excès de son destin, qui tantôt m'amoindrit et tantôt me complète, vous émergez à l'instant près de moi, dauphine, salamandre, et je ne vous suis rien.

A RENDEZVOUS IN LYON

I will come by the bridge farthest from Bellecour, allowing you to arrive first. You will lead me to the window where your eyes voyage, whence your favors plunge when your freedom exchanges its light with the light of meteors, yours remaining and theirs dying out. With my dreams, with my war, with my kiss, under the revived mulberry tree, in a respite from prying eyes, I will try to isolate your conquest of an anterior knowledge, other than mine. If the future carries you off with different lovers, I will cede, but only for the sake of the single masterpiece!

Flame surpassing its destiny, which now thins me and now completes me, you brighten beside me this very moment, dauphine, salamander, and I am nothing to you.

SUR LE TYMPAN D'UNE ÉGLISE ROMANE

Maison pour recevoir l'abandonné de Dieu,
Dos étréci et bleu de pierres.

Ah! désespoir avide d'ombre,
Indéfiniment poursuivi
Dans son amour et son squelette.

Vérité aux secrètes larmes,
La plus offrante des tanières!

ON THE TYMPANUM OF A ROMANESQUE CHURCH

House for receiving the forsaken of God,
Its back a cramped blue wall of stones.

Ah! desperation longing for shadow,
Indefinitely hounded
In his love and his skeleton.

Truth hiding its tears,
The highest bidder among hideaways!

LA LISIÈRE DU TROUBLE

Toutes les mains sur une pierre,
Les mains de pourpre et les dociles,
Pour deux actives qui distillent.

Mains, par temps sublime, que l'air fonde au même instant que l'arc;
Données par le parfum de l'iris des marais à ma lourdeur,
Un soir brumeux, de leur côté.

(Paris, Musée Rodin)

THE BOUNDARY OF UNREST

All the hands on a stone,
Furious hands and docile hands,
For two that are active and distill.

Hands that, in sublime weather, are founded by the air at the same moment
     as the arc,
Given to my heaviness by the marsh iris's scent,
An evening of fog, from their side.

(Paris, Musée Rodin)

LE VIPEREAU

Il glisse contre la mousse du caillou comme le jour cligne à travers le volet. Une goutte d'eau pourrait le coiffer, deux brindilles le revêtir. Âme en peine d'un bout de terre et d'un carré de buis, il en est, en même temps, la dent maudite et déclive. Son vis-à-vis, son adversaire, c'est le petit matin qui, après avoir tâté la courtepointe et avoir souri à la main du dormeur, lâche sa fourche et file au plafond de la chambre. Le soleil, second venu, l'embellit d'une lèvre friande.

Le vipereau restera froid jusqu'à la mort nombreuse, car, n'étant d'aucune paroisse, il est meurtrier devant toutes.

THE YOUNG SNAKE

He glides over the mossy stone as daylight flickers through a shutter. A drop of water could do his hair, two twigs could dress him. A soul longing for a patch of earth and a bit of boxwood, he is at the same time their cursed and slanted tooth. His opposite, his adversary, is the earliest dawn that, having touched the quilt and smiled at the sleeper's hand, leaves its fork and passes to the bedroom ceiling. The sun, the second to arrive, embellishes him with a delicate lip.

The little snake will remain cold till manifold death, for, belonging to no parish, he is a murderer in the eyes of all.

VERMILLON

Réponse à un peintre

Qu'elle vienne, maîtresse, à ta marche inclinée,
Ou qu'elle appelle de la brume du bois;
Qu'en sa chambre elle soit prévenue et suivie,
Épouse à son carreau, fusée inaperçue;
Sa main, fendant la mer et caressant tes doigts,
Déplace de l'été la borne invariable.

La tempête et la nuit font chanter, je l'entends,
Dans le fer de tes murs le galet d'Agrigente.

Fontainier, quel dépit de ne pouvoir tirer de son caveau mesquin
La source, notre endroit!

VERMILLION

Response to a painter

Whether she comes as a mistress to your sloping stair,
Or whether she calls from the mist of the woods;
Whether in her room she is sent word and followed,
A wife at her window, an unperceived fuse;
Her hand, rending the sea and caressing your fingers,
Displaces summer's invariable boundary stone.

Night and the storm are making the shingle of Agrigento—
I hear it—sing in the iron of your walls.

Oh unearther of springs, the frustration of not being able to draw from the
    meager shaft
The source, our place.

MARMONNEMENT

Pour ne pas me rendre et pour m'y retrouver, je t'offense, mais combien je suis épris de toi, loup, qu'on dit à tort funèbre, pétri des secrets de mon arrière-pays. C'est dans une masse d'amour légendaire que tu laisses la déchaussure vierge, pourchassée, de ton ongle. Loup, je t'appelle, mais tu n'as pas de réalité nommable. De plus, tu es inintelligible. Non-comparant, compensateur, que sais-je? Derrière ta course sans crinière, je saigne, je pleure, je m'enserre de terreur, j'oublie, je ris sous les arbres. Traque impitoyable où l'on s'acharne, où tout est mis en action contre la double proie: toi invisible et moi vivace.

Continue, va, nous durons ensemble; et ensemble, bien que séparés, nous bondissons par-dessus le frisson de la suprême déception pour briser la glace des eaux vives et se reconnaître là.

MUTTERING

To persist unsurrendering, to find my way, I offend you, but how in love with you I am, wolf, wrongly called mournful, steeped in the secrets of my back-country. It is in a mass of legendary love that you leave the virgin trace of your always pursued claw. Wolf, I call you, but you have no namable reality. What's more, you're unintelligible. Not appearing, compensatory, what could I know? Behind your maneless running I bleed, I cry, I shut myself in terror, I forget, I laugh under the trees. Pitiless, relentless chase where everything is put in action against the double prey: you invisible and I unwavering.

Go on, run, we last together; and together, though separate, we leap over the shudder of pure disappointment to shatter the ice of living waters and recognize each other there.

LE RISQUE ET LE PENDULE

Toi qui ameutes et qui passes entre l'épanouie et le voltigeur, sois celui pour qui le papillon touche les fleurs du chemin.

Reste avec la vague à la seconde où son cœur expire. Tu verras.

Sensible aussi à la salive du rameau.

Sans plus choisir entre oublier et bien apprendre.

Puisses-tu garder au vent de ta branche tes amis essentiels.

Elle transporte le verbe, l'abeille frontalière qui, à travers haines ou embuscades, va pondre son miel sur la passade d'un nuage.

La nuit ne s'étonne plus du volet que l'homme tire.

Une poussière qui tombe sur la main occupée à tracer le poème, les foudroie, poème et main.

RISK AND THE PENDULUM

You who stir commotion and pass between the blossom and the acrobat, be the one for whom the butterfly touches the flowers of the path.

Stay with the wave at the second its heart expires. You will see.

Responsive, too, to the bough's saliva.

Without choosing anymore between forgetting and learning well.

May you keep in your branch's wind your essential friends.

It carries the word, this bee of frontiers that, surviving hatreds and ambushes, will place its honey on a cloud's whim.

Night is no longer surprised by the shutter a man closes.

A dust falling on the hand engaged in tracing the poem strikes both, poem and hand, like lightning.

POUR RENOUER

Nous nous sommes soudain trop approchés de quelque chose dont on nous tenait à une distance mystérieusement favorisable et mesurée. Depuis lors, c'est le rongement. Notre appui-tête a disparu.

Il est insupportable de se sentir part solidaire et impuissante d'une beauté en train de mourir par la faute d'autrui. Solidaire dans sa poitrine et impuissant dans le mouvement de son esprit.

Si ce que je te montre et ce que je te donne te semblent moindres que ce que je te cache, ma balance est pauvre, ma glane est sans vertu.

Tu es reposoir d'obscurité sur ma face trop offerte, poème. Ma splendeur et ma souffrance se sont glissées entre les deux.

Jeter bas l'existence laidement accumulée et retrouver le regard qui l'aima assez à son début pour en étaler le fondement. Ce qui me reste à vivre est dans cet assaut, dans ce frisson.

TO RENEW

Suddenly we came too close to something that had been held at a mysteriously favorable and measured distance. Since then, it's an eating away. Our headrest has disappeared.

It's unbearable to feel oneself powerlessly in solidarity with something beautiful in the process of dying through the fault of others. In solidarity in one's heart, powerless in the movement of one's mind.

If what I show you and what I give you seem less than what I hide from you, my weighing is poor, my gleaning is without virtue.

You are an altar of darkness on my unsheltered face, poem. My splendor and my suffering have slipped between the two.

To cast off life's ugly accretions and find again the gaze that loved it enough in the beginning to display its foundation. What I have left to live lies in this fury, this shudder.

LE BOIS DE L'EPTE

Je n'étais ce jour-là que deux jambes qui marchent.
Aussi, le regard sec, le nul au centre du visage,
Je me mis à suivre le ruisseau du vallon.
Bas coureur, ce fade ermite ne s'immisçait pas
Dans l'informe où je m'étendais toujours plus avant.

Venus du mur d'angle d'une ruine laissée jadis par l'incendie,
Plongèrent soudain dans l'eau grise
Deux rosiers sauvages pleins d'une douce et inflexible volonté.
Il s'y devinait comme un commerce d'êtres disparus, à la veille de s'annoncer
    encore.

Le rauque incarnat d'une rose, en frappant l'eau,
Rétablit la face première du ciel avec l'ivresse des questions,
Éveilla au milieu des paroles amoureuses la terre,
Me poussa dans l'avenir comme un outil affamé et fiévreux.

Le bois de l'Epte commençait un tournant plus loin.
Mais je n'eus pas à le traverser, le cher grainetier du relèvement!
Je humai, sur le talon du demi-tour, le remugle des prairies où fondait une
    bête,
J'entendis glisser la peureuse couleuvre;
De chacun—ne me traitez pas durement—j'accomplissais, je le sus, les
    souhaits.

THE EPTE WOODS

I was simply two legs walking that day.
With a dry eye, a nothing at the center of my face,
I set to following the stream of the valley.
That tired hermit, a gray trickle, didn't enter
The expanse where I extended my step ever further.

From the angle of a wall long ago ruined by fire
There suddenly plunged in the water
Two wild rosebushes, full of a sweet and unbending will.
One felt there a flurry of vanished beings, about to come forth again.

The hoarse crimson of a rose, striking the water,
Restored in a rapture of questions the original face of the sky,
Awakened the earth in a space of loving words,
Thrust me into the future like a famished and feverish tool.

The Epte Woods began at the next bend.
But I didn't have to cross them, dear seedbeds of recovery!
I breathed, in turning on my heel, the smell of prairies where an animal was
    disappearing.
I heard the timid grass snake slip by.
Of everyone—don't treat me harshly—I accomplished (I was sure) the
    wishes.

VICTOIRE ÉCLAIR

L'oiseau bêche la terre,
Le serpent sème,
La mort améliorée
Applaudit la récolte.

Pluton dans le ciel!

L'explosion en nous.
Là seulement dans moi.
Fol et sourd, comment pourrais-je l'être davantage?

Plus de second soi-même, de visage changeant, plus de saison pour la flamme
et de saison pour l'ombre!

Avec la lente neige descendent les lépreux.

Soudain l'amour, l'égal de la terreur,
D'une main jamais vue arrête l'incendie, redresse le soleil, reconstruit l'Amie.

Rien n'annonçait une existence si forte.

LIGHTNING VICTORY

The bird turns the earth,
The serpent sows,
Death improved
Celebrates the harvest.

Pluto in the sky!

The explosion in us.
There solely in me.
Mad and deaf, how could I be more so?

No more second self, changing face, no more season for the flame and season
   for the shadow!

The lepers come down with the slowly falling snow.

Suddenly love, the equal of terror,
With a hand never before seen halts the blaze, straightens the sun, composes
   the Beloved anew.

Nothing foretold so strong an existence.

LA CHAMBRE DANS L'ESPACE

Tel le chant du ramier quand l'averse est prochaine—l'air se poudre de pluie, de soleil revenant—, je m'éveille lavé, je fonds en m'élevant; je vendange le ciel novice.

Allongé contre toi, je meus ta liberté. Je suis un bloc de terre qui réclame sa fleur.

Est-il gorge menuisée plus radieuse que la tienne? Demander c'est mourir!

L'aile de ton soupir met un duvet aux feuilles. Le trait de mon amour ferme ton fruit, le boit.

Je suis dans la grâce de ton visage que mes ténèbres couvrent de joie.

Comme il est beau ton cri qui me donne ton silence!

THE ROOM IN SPACE

Like the dove's song when the shower is near—the air is powdered with rain, with sifted light—I awaken washed, I melt in rising; I harvest the early sky.

Lying at your side, I move your freedom. I am a portion of earth that claims its flower.

Is there a delicate throat more radiant than yours? To ask is to die!

The wing of your sigh places bird's down on the leaves. The act of my love completes your fruit, drinks it.

I live in the grace of your gaze that my darkness covers with joy.

How beautiful your cry that gives me your silence!

RAPPORT DE MARÉE

Terre et ciel ont-ils renoncé à leurs féeries saisonnières, à leur palabres subtiles? Se sont-ils soumis? Pas plus celle-ci que celui-là n'ont encore, il semble, de projets pour eux, de bonheur pour nous.

Une branche s'éveille aux paroles dorées de la lampe, une branche dans une eau fade, un rameau sans avenir. Le regard s'en saisit, voyage. Puis, de nouveau, tout languit, patiente, se balance et souffre. L'acanthe simule la mort. Mais, cette fois, nous ne ferons pas route ensemble.

Bien-aimée, derrière ma porte?

REPORT ON THE TIDE

Have earth and sky abandoned their seasons of enchantment, their subtle conversations? Have they submitted? Neither, it seems, any longer has plans for the two of them, happiness for us.

A branch awakes to the lamp's gold words, a branch in dull water, a bough without a future. The eye captures it, voyages. Then, again, everything is left to languish, wait, waver, suffer. The acanthus imitates death. But this time we won't travel together.

Beloved, behind my door?

INVITATION

J'appelle les amours qui roués et suivis par la faulx de l'été, au soir embaument l'air de leur blanche inaction.

Il n'y a plus de cauchemar, douce insomnie perpétuelle. Il n'y a plus d'aversion. Que la pause d'un bal dont l'entrée est partout dans les nuées du ciel.

Je viens avant la rumeur des fontaines, au final du tailleur de pierre.

Sur ma lyre mille ans pèsent moins qu'un mort.

J'appelle les amants.

INVITATION

I call the loves that, racked and chased by summer's scythe, at evening embalm the air with their white inaction.

There is no more nightmare, soft perpetual insomnia. There is no more aversion. Only the pause of a dance that can be entered anywhere in the clouds crossing the sky.

I come before the murmur of fountains, at the carver's final stone.

On my lyre a thousand years weigh less than a dead man.

I call the lovers.

POURQUOI LA JOURNÉE VOLE

Le poète s'appuie, durant le temps de sa vie, à quelque arbre, ou mer, ou talus, ou nuage d'une certaine teinte, un moment, si la circonstance le veut. Il n'est pas soudé à l'égarement d'autrui. Son amour, son saisir, son bonheur ont leur équivalent dans tous les lieux où il n'est pas allé, où jamais il n'ira, chez les étrangers qu'il ne connaîtra pas. Lorsqu'on élève la voix devant lui, qu'on le presse d'accepter des égards qui retiennent, si l'on invoque à son propos les astres, il répond qu'il est du pays d'*à côté*, du ciel qui vient d'être englouti.

Le poète vivifie puis court au dénouement.

Au soir, malgré sur sa joue plusieurs fossettes d'apprenti, c'est un passant courtois qui brusque les adieux pour être là quand le pain sort du four.

WHY THE DAY FLIES

The poet, throughout his life, leans for a moment against some tree, or sea, or bank of earth, or cloud of a certain hue, as circumstances permit. He is not fused to the distractions of others. His love, his joy, his astonished reach have their equivalent in all the places he has not gone, all the places he will never go, among strangers he will not know. When we lift our voices to him, when we greet him with honors that bind, if we invoke the stars in his name, he responds that he is from the country *beside*, from the sky that has just gone under.

The poet quickens, then runs to the outcome.

At evening, despite the apprentice's dimples on his cheeks, he is a courteous passerby whose farewells are brief so he can be there when the bread comes out of the oven.

LA BIBLIOTHÈQUE EST EN FEU
ET AUTRES POÈMES

THE LIBRARY IS ON FIRE
AND OTHER POEMS

LA BIBLIOTHÈQUE EST EN FEU

À Georges Braque

Par la bouche de ce canon il neige. C'était l'enfer dans notre tête. Au même moment c'est le printemps au bout de nos doigts. C'est la foulée de nouveau permise, la terre en amour, les herbes exubérantes.

L'esprit aussi, comme toute chose, a tremblé.

L'aigle est au futur.

Toute action qui engage l'âme, quand bien même celle-ci serait ignorante, aura pour épilogue un repentir ou un chagrin. Il faut y consentir.

Comment me vint l'écriture? Comme un duvet d'oiseau sur ma vitre, en hiver. Aussitôt s'éleva dans l'âtre une bataille de tisons qui n'a pas, encore à présent, pris fin.

Soyeuses villes du regard quotidien, insérées parmi d'autres villes, aux rues tracées par nous seuls, sous l'aile d'éclairs qui répondent à nos attentions.

Tout en nous ne devrait être qu'une fête joyeuse quand quelque chose que nous n'avons pas prévu, que nous n'éclairons pas, qui va parler à notre cœur, par ses seuls moyens, s'accomplit.

Continuons à jeter nos coups de sonde, à parler à voix égale, par mots groupés, nous finirons par faire taire tous ces chiens, par obtenir qu'ils se confondent avec l'herbage, nous surveillant d'un œil fumeux, tandis que le vent effacera leur dos.

L'éclair me dure.

Il n'y a que mon semblable, la compagne ou le compagnon, qui puisse m'éveiller de ma torpeur, déclencher la poésie, me lancer contre les limites du vieux désert afin que j'en triomphe. Aucun autre. Ni cieux, ni terre privilégiée, ni choses dont on tressaille.
Torche, je ne valse qu'avec lui.

THE LIBRARY IS ON FIRE

To Georges Braque

Through this cannon mouth it's snowing. It was hell in our head. At the same time it's spring at our fingertips. It's the long stride allowed again, the earth in love, the exuberant grass.

The mind too, like all things, has trembled.

The eagle belongs to the future.

Every action that commits the soul, even when the soul is unaware of it, has for an epilogue either a repentance or a grief. One must consent to this.

How did writing come to me? Like bird's down on my window, in winter. Immediately there arose in the hearth a battle of embers that has not, thus far, come to an end.

Silken cities of our daily gaze, inserted among other cities, with streets drawn by us alone, under the wing of lightning flashes that respond to our attentions.

Everything within us should be a joyous celebration when something we haven't foreseen, that we do not clarify, that's going to speak to our heart, is by its own means realized.

Let us continue to cast our soundings, to speak in a steady voice, in gathered words. We will end by silencing all these dogs, making them blend with the pasture, where they watch us with smoky eyes as the wind begins to obliterate their backs.

The lightning lasts me.

Only my companion, she or he, can awaken me from my torpor, releasing poetry, launching me against the limits of the old desert so that I can overcome it. No other. Neither the heavens, nor a privileged place, nor the things by which we are shaken.

Torch, I dance only with a companion like this.

On ne peut pas commencer un poème sans une parcelle d'erreur sur soi et sur le monde, sans une paille d'innocence aux premiers mots.

Dans le poème, chaque mot ou presque doit être employé dans son sens originel. Certains, se détachant, deviennent plurivalents. Il en est d'amnésiques. La constellation du Solitaire est tendue.

La poésie me volera ma mort.

Pourquoi *poème pulvérisé*? Parce qu'au terme de son voyage vers le Pays, après l'obscurité pré-natale et la dureté terrestre, la finitude du poème est lumière, apport de l'être à la vie.

Le poète ne retient pas ce qu'il découvre; l'ayant transcrit, le perd bientôt. En cela résident sa nouveauté, son infini et son péril.

Mon métier est un métier de pointe.

On naît avec les hommes, on meurt inconsolé parmi les dieux.

La terre qui reçoit la graine est triste. La graine qui va tant risquer est heureuse.

Il est une malédiction qui ne ressemble à aucune autre. Elle papillote dans une sorte de paresse, a une nature avenante, se compose un visage aux traits rassurants. Mais quel ressort, passée la feinte, quelle course immédiate au but! Probablement, car l'ombre où elle échafaude est maligne, la région parfaitement secrète, elle se soustraira à une appellation, s'esquivera toujours à temps. Elle dessine dans le voile du ciel de quelques clairvoyants des paraboles assez effrayantes.

Livres sans mouvement. Mais livres qui s'introduisent avec souplesse dans nos jours, y poussent une plainte, ouvrent des bals.

Comment dire ma liberté, ma surprise, au terme de mille détours: il n'y a pas de fond, il n'y a pas de plafond.

One cannot begin a poem without a particle of error about oneself and about the world, without a straw of innocence in the first words.

In the poem, almost every word must be used in its original sense. Some, coming free, turn plurivalent. Some are without memory. The constellation of the Solitary is extended.

Poetry will steal my death.

Why *pulverized poem*? Because at the end of its voyage toward the Land, after the prenatal darkness and the terrestrial harshness, the finitude of the poem is light, the gift of being to life.

The poet doesn't keep what he discovers; having written it down, he soon loses it. In this resides his newness, his infinite, his peril.

My métier, at the cutting edge, is a métier of point.

We are born with men, we die unconsoled among gods.

The earth that receives the grain is sad. The grain that's going to risk so much is happy.

There is a curse unlike any other. It flutters about in a sort of laziness, has a welcoming nature, composes a face with reassuring features. But, after the feint, what power, what sudden flight to the goal! Probably, as the shadow where it builds is cunning, the region perfectly secret, it will elude a name, will always slip away in time. It sketches, in the veil of the sky of a few clairvoyants, quite frightening parabolas.

Books without movement. But books that work their way into our lives with suppleness, begin a lament there, open places for dances.

How to speak of my freedom, my surprise, at the end of a thousand detours: there is no floor, there is no ceiling.

Parfois la silhouette d'un jeune cheval, d'un enfant lointain, s'avance en éclaireur vers mon front et saute la barre de mon souci. Alors sous les arbres reparle la fontaine.

Nous désirons rester inconnus à la curiosité de celles qui nous aiment. Nous les aimons.

La lumière a un âge. La nuit n'en a pas. Mais quel fut l'instant de cette source entière?

Ne pas avoir plusieurs morts suspendues et comme enneigées. N'en avoir qu'une, de bon sable. Et sans résurrection.

Arrêtons-nous près des êtres qui peuvent se couper de leurs ressources, bien qu'il n'existe pour eux que peu ou pas de repli. L'attente leur creuse une insomnie vertigineuse. La beauté leur pose un chapeau de fleurs.

Oiseaux qui confiez votre gracilité, votre sommeil périlleux à un ramas de roseaux, le froid venu, comme nous vous ressemblons!

J'admire les mains qui emplissent, et, pour apparier, pour joindre, le doigt qui refuse le dé.

Je m'avise parfois que le courant de notre existence est peu saisissable, puisque nous subissons non seulement sa faculté capricieuse, mais le facile mouvement des bras et des jambes qui nous ferait aller là où nous serions heureux d'aller, sur la rive convoitée, à la rencontre d'amours dont les différences nous enrichiraient, ce mouvement demeure inaccompli, vite déclinant en image, comme un parfum en boule sur notre pensée.

Désir, désir qui sait, nous ne tirons avantage de nos ténèbres qu'à partir de quelques souverainetés véritables assorties d'invisibles flammes, d'invisibles chaînes, qui, se révélant, pas après pas, nous font briller.

La beauté fait son lit sublime toute seule, étrangement bâtit sa renommée parmi les hommes, à côté d'eux mais à l'écart.

Semons les roseaux et cultivons la vigne sur les coteaux, au bord des plaies de notre esprit. Doigts cruels, mains précautionneuses, ce lieu facétieux est propice.

Sometimes the silhouette of a young horse, of a distant child, approaches my forehead like a guide and leaps the barrier of my worry. Then the fountain speaks again under the trees.

We wish to remain unknown to the curiosity of those who love us. We love them.

The light has an age. The night doesn't. But what was the moment of this entire source?

Not to have several suspended and, as it were, snow-covered deaths. To have only one, of good sand, and without resurrection.

Let us halt near those who can cut themselves off from their resources, though there exists little or no space of withdrawal for them. Waiting digs for them a vertiginous insomnia. Beauty lays upon them a hat of flowers.

Birds that entrust your slenderness, your perilous sleep, to a stand of reeds when the cold is come, how we resemble you!

I admire hands that fill, and, for matching, for joining, the finger that refuses the thimble.

Sometimes it occurs to me that the current of our existence is barely perceptible, for we suffer not only its capricious power, but also the fluent movement of arms and legs that would make us go where we'd be happy going, the shore we've longed for, the encounters of love where the differences would be our deepening. This movement remains unaccomplished, quickly declining into an image, like a scent rolled up in a ball above our thought.

Desire, ah desire that knows, we make use of our darkness only on the basis of a few genuine sovereignties bearing invisible flames, invisible chains, which, in revealing themselves, step by step, make us shine.

Beauty makes its sublime bed all alone, strangely builds its fame among men, beside them but off the path.

Let us sow reeds and cultivate the vine on the hills, on the borders of the mind's wounds. Cruel fingers, careful hands, this place of mischief is promising.

Celui qui invente, au contraire de celui qui découvre, n'ajoute aux choses, n'apporte aux êtres que des masques, des entre-deux, une bouillie de fer.

Enfin toute la vie, quand j'arrache la douceur de ta vérité amoureuse à ton profond!

Restez près du nuage. Veillez près de l'outil. Toute semence est détestée.

Bienfaisance des hommes certains matins stridents. Dans le fourmillement de l'air en délire, je monte, je m'enferme, insecte indévoré, suivi et poursuivant.

Face à ces eaux, de formes dures, où passent en bouquets éclatés toutes les fleurs de la montagne verte, les Heures épousent des dieux.

Frais soleil dont je suis la liane.

He who invents, as opposed to he who discovers, doesn't add to things, doesn't bring to beings anything but masks, lace inserts, a pulp of iron.

At last the whole of life, when I wrest the sweetness of your loving truth from your depth!

Stay near the cloud. Keep watch near the tool. All seeds are detested.

The charity of men on certain raucous mornings. In the swarming of air in delirium, I climb, I enclose myself, undevoured insect, pursued and pursuing.

Facing these severe waters, where all the flowers of the green mountain go by in shattered bouquets, the Hours marry gods.

Fresh sun of which I am the liana.

LES COMPAGNONS DANS LE JARDIN

L'homme n'est qu'une fleur de l'air tenue par la terre, maudite par les astres, respirée par la mort; le souffle et l'ombre de cette coalition, certaines fois, le surélèvent.

Notre amitié est le nuage blanc préféré du soleil.

Notre amitié est une écorce libre. Elle ne se détache pas des prouesses de notre cœur.

Où l'esprit ne déracine plus mais replante et soigne, je nais. Où commence l'enfance du peuple, j'aime.

XXe siècle: l'homme fut au plus bas. Les femmes s'éclairaient et se déplaçaient vite, sur un surplomb où seuls nos yeux avaient accès.

À une rose je me lie.

Nous sommes ingouvernables. Le seul maître qui nous soit propice, c'est l'Éclair, qui tantôt nous illumine et tantôt nous pourfend.

Éclair et rose, en nous, dans leur fugacité, pour nous accomplir, s'ajoutent.

Je suis d'herbe dans ta main, ma pyramide adolescente. Je t'aime sur tes milles fleurs refermées.

Prête au bourgeon, en lui laissant l'avenir, tout l'éclat de la fleur profonde. Ton dur second regard le peut. De la sorte, le gel ne le détruira pas.

Ne permettons pas qu'on nous enlève la part de la nature que nous renfermons. N'en perdons pas une étamine, n'en cédons pas un gravier d'eau.

Après le départ des moissonneurs, sur les plateaux de l'Ile-de-France, ce menu silex taillé qui sort de terre, à peine dans notre main, fait surgir de notre mémoire un noyau équivalent, noyau d'une aurore dont nous ne verrons pas, croyons-nous, l'altération ni la fin; seulement la rougeur sublime et le visage levé.

COMPANIONS IN THE GARDEN

Man is only a flower of the air, held by the earth, cursed by the stars, inhaled by death; the breath and shadow of this alliance, at moments, raise him higher.

Our friendship is the white cloud the sun prefers.

Our friendship is the bark on a tree of freedom. It does not come loose from the actions of our heart.

Where the mind no longer uproots but plants and tends, I am born. Where the childhood of a people begins, I love.

The twentieth century: man was at his basest. Women brightened and moved quickly, on an overhang that only our eyes could reach.

To a rose I bind myself.

We are ungovernable. The only master auspicious for us is the Lightning, which now illumines us, now rends us.

The lightning and the rose, in their fleetingness, come together in us, complete us.

I'm the grass in your hand, my adolescent pyramid. I love you in your thousand enfolded flowers.

Lend to the bud, in leaving it the future, all the brightness of the deep flower. Your firm second look can do it. In this way the frost will not destroy it.

Let us not allow them to take away that part of nature we hold within. Let us not lose the smallest stamen of it, not cede a single riverbed stone of it.

After the departure of the harvesters, on the plateaus of the Ile-de-France, this slender carved flint poking through the ground, once placed in our hands, releases in memory an equivalent core, the core of a dawn of which we believe we will see neither an alteration nor an end: only the sublime redness and the raised face.

Leur crime: un enragé vouloir de nous apprendre à mépriser les dieux que nous avons en nous.

Ce sont les pessimistes que l'avenir élève. Ils voient de leur vivant l'objet de leur appréhension se réaliser. Pourtant la grappe, qui a suivi la moisson, au-dessus de son cep, boucle; et les enfants des saisons, qui ne sont pas selon l'ordinaire réunis, au plus vite affermissent le sable au bord de la vague. Cela, les pessimistes le perçoivent aussi.

Ah! le pouvoir de se lever autrement.

Dites, ce que nous sommes nous fera jaillir en bouquet?

Un poète doit laisser des traces de son passage, non des preuves. Seules les traces font rêver.

Vivre, c'est s'obstiner à achever un souvenir? Mourir, c'est devenir, mais nulle part, vivant?

Le réel quelquefois désaltère l'espérance. C'est pourquoi, contre toute attente, l'espérance survit.

Toucher de son ombre un fumier, tant notre flanc renferme de maux et notre cœur de pensées folles, se peut; mais avoir en soi un sacré.

Lorsque je rêve et que j'avance, lorsque je retiens l'ineffable, m'éveillant, je suis à genoux.

L'Histoire n'est que le revers de la tenue des maîtres. Aussi une terre d'effroi où chasse le lycaon et que racle la vipère. La détresse est dans le regard des sociétés humaines et du Temps, avec des victoires qui montent.

Luire et s'élancer—prompt couteau, lente étoile.

Dans l'éclatement de l'univers que nous éprouvons, prodige! les morceaux qui s'abattent sont vivants.

Ma toute terre, comme un oiseau changé en fruit dans un arbre éternel, je suis à toi.

Their crime: an enraged will to teach us to despise the gods we have within.

These are the pessimists the future raises. In the course of their lives they see their apprehensions come to pass. Yet the grape cluster that has followed the harvest, above its stock, bends; and the children of the seasons, not ordinarily gathered together, quickly pack the sand at the edge of the wave. That, too, pessimists perceive.

Ah! the power to rise in the morning otherwise.

Tell me, what we are, will it make us spring forth like a bouquet?

A poet should leave traces of his passage, not proofs. Only traces stir our dreaming.

Is to live to persevere in finishing a recollection? Is to die to become, nowhere at all, alive?

The real sometimes satisfies hope. That's why hope, against all expectation, survives.

Our shadow will now and then fall in the filth, given all the ills in our body, all the mad thoughts in our heart; yet to keep within oneself something sacred.

When I dream and go forward, when I hold the ineffable, awakening, I'm on my knees.

History is but the underside of the manners of masters. As well as an earth of terror where the lycaon hunts, that the viper scrapes. Suffering is in the gaze of human societies and of Time, with victories that rise.

To gleam and to leap—quick knife, slow star.

In the shattering of the universe that we experience—O miracle!—the pieces in collapse are alive.

My entire earth, like a bird changed into fruit in an eternal tree, I belong to you.

Ce que vos hivers nous demandent, c'est d'enlever dans les airs ce qui ne serait sans cela que limaille et souffre-douleur. Ce que vos hivers nous demandent, c'est de préluder pour vous à la saveur: une saveur égale à celle que chante sous sa rondeur ailée la civilisation du fruit.

Ce qui me console, lorsque je serai mort, c'est que je serai là—disloqué, hideux—pour me voir poème.

Il ne faut pas que ma lyre me devine, que mon vers se trouve ce que j'aurais pu écrire.

Le merveilleux chez cet être: toute source, en lui, donne le jour à un ruisseau. Avec le moindre de ses dons descend une averse de colombes.

Dans nos jardins se préparent des forêts.

Les oiseaux libres ne souffrent pas qu'on les regarde. Demeurons obscurs, renonçons à nous, près d'eux.

Ô survie encore, toujours meilleure!

What your winters demand is that we clear away in air that which, otherwise, would be only iron filings and scapegoats. What your winters demand is that we presage for you a savor: a savor equal to that which the civilization of fruit sings in its winged fullness.

What consoles me, when I think of being dead, is that I will be there— disjointed, hideous—to see myself poem.

Why should my lyre guess me, or my poem turn out to be that which I could have written?

The marvelous aspect of this person: every source, in him, gives birth to a stream. With the least of his gifts a shower of doves descends.

In our gardens, forests are prepared.

Birds that are free cannot bear to be watched. Let us remain obscure, let us renounce ourselves, near them.

O life surviving still, always better!

BONNE GRÂCE D'UN TEMPS D'AVRIL

À une enfant

Hélène,
Au lent berceau, au doux cheval,
Bonjour! Mon auberge est la tienne.

Comme ta chaleur est adroite
Qui sait, en biais, m'atteindre au cœur,
Enfant chérie des ruisseaux, des rêveurs,
Hélène! Hélène!

Mais que te veulent les saisons
Qui t'aiment de quatre manières?
Que ta beauté, cette lumière,
Entre et passe en chaque maison?
Ou, que la lune à jamais grande
Te tienne et t'entoure la main
Jusqu'à l'amour que tu demandes?

THE GOOD GRACE OF AN APRIL DAY

To a child

Hélène,
Of the patient cradle, the gentle horse,
Good afternoon! My inn is yours.

How lithe and agile your warmth
That's able to reach my heart at an angle,
Child adored by brooks, by dreamers,
Hélène, Hélène!

But what do the seasons wish you,
Loving you in their four ways?
That the light of your beauty
Should enter and pass through each house?
That the moon forever large
Should hold you and circle your hand
All the way to the love you seek?

LA PASSANTE DE SCEAUX

Mèches, au dire du regard,
Désir simple de parole;
Ah! jongle, seigneurie du cou
Avec la souveraine bouche,
Avec le bûcher allumé
Au-dessous du front dominant.

J'aimerais savoir vous mentir
Comme le tison ment aux cendres,
Mèches, qui volez sans m'entendre
Sur le théâtre d'un instant.

L'ARBRE FRAPPÉ

I

Enlevé par l'oiseau à l'éparse douleur,
Et laissé aux forêts pour un travail d'amour.

II

La foudre spacieuse et le feu du baiser
Charmeront mon tombeau par l'orage dressé.

THE PASSERBY OF SCEAUX

Loose hair, in the light of the eyes,
A simple desire to speak;
Ah, balance, noble curve of the neck,
With the sovereign mouth,
With the ardent stake glowing
Behind the prominent forehead.

I'd love to be able to lie to you
As the brand deceives the ashes,
Loose hair, unlistening, that flies
Through the theater of a moment.

THE TREE STRUCK BY LIGHTNING

I

Collected by a bird from the scattered grief,
Left to the forests for a work of love.

II

The spacious lightning and the fire of the kiss
Will charm my tomb that the storm has raised.

NEUF MERCI POUR VIEIRA DA SILVA

I

LES PALAIS ET LES MAISONS

Paris est aujourd'hui achevé. J'y vivrai. Mon bras ne lance plus mon âme au loin. J'appartiens.

II

DANS L'ESPACE

Le soleil volait bas, aussi bas que l'oiseau. La nuit les éteignit tous deux. Je les aimais.

III

C'EST BIEN ELLE

Terre de basse nuit et des harcèlements.

*

Nuit, mon feuillage et ma glèbe.

IV

LA GRILLE

Je ne suis pas seul parce que je suis abandonné. Je suis seul parce que je suis seul, amande entre les parois de sa closerie.

NINE THANKS FOR VIEIRA DA SILVA

I

THE PALACES AND THE HOUSES

Paris today is brought to a close. This is where I'll live. My arm no longer launches my soul into the distance. I belong.

II

IN SPACE

The sun flew low, low as a bird. Night extinguished the two of them. I loved them.

III

SO LIKE HER

Earth of low night and vexings.

*

Night, my foliage and my plot of land.

IV

THE GATE

I'm not alone because I'm abandoned. I'm alone because I'm alone, almond between the walls of its shell.

V

Les dieux sont de retour, compagnons. Ils viennent à l'instant de pénétrer dans cette vie; mais la parole qui révoque, sous la parole qui déploie, est réapparue, elle aussi, pour ensemble nous faire souffrir.

VI

ARTINE DANS L'ÉCHO

Notre emmêlement somptueux dans le corps de la voie lactée, chambre au sommet pour notre couple qui dans la nuit ailleurs se glacerait.

VII

BERCEUSE POUR CHAQUE JOUR
JUSQU'AU DERNIER

Nombreuses fois, nombre de fois,
L'homme s'endort, son corps l'éveille;
Puis une fois, rien qu'une fois,
L'homme s'endort et perd son corps.

VIII

AUX MIENS

Je touche à l'étendue et je peux l'enflammer. Je retiens ma largeur, je sais la déployer. Mais que vaut le désir sans votre essaim jaloux? Terne est le bouton d'or sans le ton des prairies.

Lorsque vous surgirez, ma main vous requerra, ma main, le petit monstre resté vif. Mais, à la réserve de vous, quelle beauté? . . . quelle beauté?

V

THE GODS ARE BACK

The gods are back, companions. They've just now entered this life around us; but the word that revokes, under the word that unfurls, that too has reappeared, the one with the other to make us suffer.

VI

ARTINE IN ECHO

Our sumptuous entwining in the body of the Milky Way, a room at the summit for the two of us, who otherwise would freeze in the night.

VII

LULLABY FOR EVERY DAY UNTIL THE LAST

Numerous times, a number of times,
A man sleeps, his body wakes him;
And then one time, but a single time,
A man sleeps, his body leaves him.

VIII

TO THOSE WHO ARE MINE

I touch the expanse and can set it on fire. I hold back my breadth, I know how to unfold it. But what's desire worth without your jealous swarm? Lifeless is the buttercup without the pitch of prairies.

When you appear, my hand will demand you, my hand, little monster quick as ever. But, except for you, what beauty? . . . what beauty?

IX

L'arbre le plus exposé à l'œil du fusil n'est pas un arbre pour son aile. La remuante est prévenue: elle se fera muette en le traversant. La perche de saule happée est à l'instant cédée par l'ongle de la fugitive. Mais dans la touffe de roseaux où elle amerrit, quelles cavatines! C'est ici qu'elle chante. Le monde entier le sait.

Été, rivière, espaces, amants dissimulés, toute une lune d'eau, la fauvette répète: «Libre, libre, libre, libre . . . »

IX

THE WARBLER IN THE REEDS

The tree exposed to the rifle's eye is not the tree for the warbler's wing. The restless one is warned: she will go silent when passing through. The perch in the willow is at one and the same time grasped and abandoned by the fugitive's claw. But in the cluster of reeds where she lands, what cavatinas! It's here she sings. The whole world knows it.

Summer, river, spaces, hidden lovers, an entire water moon, the warbler repeats: "free, free, free, free . . . "

DÉBRIS MORTELS ET MOZART

Au petit jour, une seule fois, le vieux nuage rose dépeuplé survolera les yeux désormais distants, dans la majesté de sa lenteur libre; puis ce sera le froid, l'immense occupant, puis le Temps qui n'a pas d'endroit.

Sur la longueur de ses deux lèvres, en terre commune, soudain l'allégro, défi de ce rebut sacré, perce et reflue vers les vivants, vers la totalité des hommes et des femmes en deuil de patrie intérieure qui, errant pour n'être pas semblables, vont à travers Mozart s'éprouver en secret.

—Bien-aimée, lorsque tu rêves à haute voix, et d'aventure prononces mon nom, tendre vainqueur de nos frayeurs conjuguées, de mon décri solitaire, la nuit est claire à traverser.

MORTAL REMAINS AND MOZART

At dawn, a single time, the old pink cloud, depleted, will drift in its free leisurely majesty over the eyes now distant; then the cold will come, immense occupying force, then Time that has no place.

Along the line of his two lips, in common earth, suddenly the allegro, defiant force of this sacred husk, breaks through and flows back toward the living, toward all the men and women who, mourning an interior country, roaming in order to be unlike all the others, will in secret test themselves through Mozart.

—Oh my love, when you dream aloud and by chance pronounce my name, tender conqueror of our combined fears, of my solitary disparagement, the night is clear to be crossed.

LE DEUIL DES NÉVONS

Pour un violon, une flûte et un écho.

Un pas de jeune fille
A caressé l'allée,
A traversé la grille.

Dans le parc des Névons
Les sauterelles dorment.
Gelée blanche et grêlons
Introduisent l'automne.

C'est le vent qui décide
Si les feuilles seront
À terre avant les nids.

*

Vite! Le souvenir néglige
Qui lui posa ce front,
Ce large coup d'œil, cette verse,
Balancement de méduse
Au-dessus du temps profond.

Il est l'égal des verveines,
Chaque été coupées ras,
Le temps où la terre sème.

*

La fenêtre et le parc,
Le platane et le toit
Lançaient charges d'abeilles,
Du pollen au rayon,
De l'essaim à la fleur.

MOURNING FOR NÉVONS

For a violin, a flute, and an echo

The step of a young girl
Has caressed the lane,
Has passed through the gate.

In the park at Névons
The grasshoppers sleep.
Frost and hail
Tell the coming of autumn.

It's the wind that decides
Whether the leaves or the nests
Will fall to the ground first.

     *

Quick! The recollection omits
Who gave it this countenance,
This broad glance, this torrent,
The swaying of a jellyfish
Above deepened time.

It's the same as verbena,
Every summer cut bare,
The time of earth's abundance.

     *

The window and the park,
The plane tree and the roof
Launched charges of bees
From the pollen to the light,
From the swarm to the flower.

Un libre oiseau voilier,
Planant pour se nourrir,
Proférait des paroles
Comme un hardi marin.

Quand le lit se fermait
Sur tout mon corps fourbu,
De beaux yeux s'en allaient
De l'ouvrage vers moi.

L'aiguille scintillait;
Et je sentais le fil
Dans le trésor des doigts
Qui brodaient la batiste.

Ah! lointain est cet âge.
Que d'années à grandir,
Sans père pour mon bras!

Tous ses dons répandus,
La rivière chérie
Subvenait aux besoins.
Peupliers et guitares
Ressuscitaient au soir
Pour fêter ce prodige
Où le ciel n'avait part.

Un faucheur de prairie
S'élevant, se voûtant,
Piquait les hirondelles,
Sans fin silencieux.

Sa quille retenue
Au limon de l'îlot,
Une barque était morte.

A seabird soaring free,
Hovering for food,
Uttered words as brazen
As the words of a sailor.

When the bed embraced
My whole exhausted body
Beautiful eyes slipped away
From the handwork toward me.

The needle was shining;
And I could feel the thread
In the treasure of the fingers
Embroidering the batiste.

Ah! how distant that time.
So many years of growing up,
Without a father at my side.

Scattering its gifts,
The cherished river
Took care of our needs.
Poplars and guitars
Were revived in the evening
To celebrate a miracle
Where heaven had no part.

A mower of the meadow
Rising, bending,
Was stirring the swallows
In endless silence.

Its keel tied
To the island's mud,
The skiff was dead.

L'heure entre classe et nuit,
La ronce les serrant,
Des garnements confus
Couraient, cruels et sourds.
La brume les sautait,
De glace et maternelle.
Sur le bambou des jungles
Ils s'étaient modelés,
Chers roseaux voltigeants!

*

Le jardinier invalide sourit
Au souvenir de ses outils perdus
Au bois mort qui se multiplie.

*

Le bien qu'on se partage,
Volonté d'un défunt,
A broyé et détruit
La pelouse et les arbres,
La paresse endormie,
L'espace ténébreux
De mon parc des Névons.

Puisqu'il faut renoncer
À ce qu'on ne peut retenir,
Qui devient autre chose
Contre ou avec le cœur,—
L'oublier rondement,

Puis battre les buissons
Pour chercher sans trouver
Ce qui doit nous guérir
De nos maux inconnus
Que nous portons partout.

In the hours between school and night,
With the brambles brushing against them,
The ragtag impish young,
Cruel and deaf, went running.
A frigid maternal mist
Drifted over their bodies.
They adopted as their models
The bamboo grasses of the jungle.
Dear fluttering reeds!

                *

The disabled gardener is smiling
At the memory of his lost tools,
At the dead wood accumulating.

                *

The gift divided
By a dead man's wish
Has crushed and destroyed
The lawn and the trees,
The dozing idleness,
The shadowed spaces
Of my park at Névons.

Since one has to renounce
That which can't be kept,
Which turns into something else,
Whatever the wish of the heart—
Wholly forget it,

Then thrash and thrash the bushes
To seek if never to find
The thing that is meant to heal us
Of all these unknown ills
We carry wherever we go.

L'UNE ET L'AUTRE

Qu'as-tu à te balancer sans fin, rosier, par longue pluie, avec ta double rose?
Comme deux guêpes mûres elles restent sans vol.
Je les vois de mon cœur car mes yeux sont fermés.
Mon amour au-dessus des fleurs n'a laissé que vent et nuage.

THE ONE AND THE OTHER

Ah, rosebush, why do you endlessly sway, through long rains, with your
    double rose?
They are like two aging wasps that have yet to take flight.
I see them from my heart, for my eyes are closed.
My love above the flowers has left but wind and cloud.

AIGUILLON

—Pourquoi cette ardeur, jeune face?
—Je pars, l'été s'efface.
À grands traits ma peur me le dit,
Mieux que l'eau grise et que les branches.
—Genoux aux poings, ange averti;
Sur ton aile mon fouet claque.

SPUR

—Why this ardor, young face?
—I'm departing, summer is vanishing.
Flashes of fear tell me this
Better than the gray water and the boughs.
—Knees like fists, ready angel:
It's on your wing we're riding now.

SUR UNE NUIT SANS ORNEMENT

Regarder la nuit battue à mort; continuer à nous suffire en elle.

Dans la nuit, le poète, le drame et la nature ne font qu'un, mais en montée et s'aspirant.

La nuit porte nourriture, le soleil affine la partie nourrie.

Dans la nuit se tiennent nos apprentissages en état de servir à d'autres, après nous. Fertile est la fraîcheur de cette gardienne!

L'infini attaque mais un nuage sauve.

La nuit s'affilie à n'importe quelle instance de la vie disposée à finir en printemps, à voler par tempête.

La nuit se colore de rouille quand elle consent à nous entrouvrir les grilles de ses jardins.

Au regard de la nuit vivante, le rêve n'est parfois qu'un lichen spectral.

Il ne fallait pas embraser le cœur de la nuit. Il fallait que l'obscur fût maître où se cisèle la rosée du matin.

La nuit ne succède qu'à elle. Le beffroi solaire n'est qu'une tolérance intéressée de la nuit.

La reconduction de notre mystère, c'est la nuit qui en prend soin; la toilette des élus, c'est la nuit qui l'exécute.

La nuit déniaise notre passé d'homme, incline sa psyché devant le présent, met de l'indécision dans notre avenir.

Je m'emplirai d'une terre céleste.

Nuit plénière où le rêve malgracieux ne clignote plus, garde-moi vivant ce que j'aime.

OF AN UNADORNED NIGHT

To see the night lashed to death; to remain self-sufficient in the night.

At night, the poet and drama and nature form a whole, in rising and inhaling one another.

Night bears nourishment, daylight sharpens the nourished part.

In the depths of night our apprenticeships are held in a condition to serve others, after us. Fertile is the cool air of this guardian.

The infinite attacks but a cloud saves.

Night affiliates itself with any phase of life ready to end in spring, to fly through storm.

Night turns rust-colored when it comes to half-open the gates of its gardens for us.

In the eyes of living night, dream is sometimes merely a spectral lichen.

There was no need to set fire to the heart of night. Darkness had to be the power where the morning's dew is carved.

Night succeeds only itself. The solar belfry is only a partial concession of night.

It's night that sees to the renewal of our mystery, that carries out the bathing of the initiates.

Night does away with our naïve human past, tilts its psyche to the present, places a measure of indecision in our future.

I will fill myself with a celestial earth.

Plenary night where ungainly dream no longer blinks, keep alive for me all that I love.

AU-DESSUS DU VENT

ABOVE THE WIND

QUATRE-DE-CHIFFRE

I
ATTENANTS

Les prairies me disent ruisseau
Et les ruisseaux prairie.

Le vent reste au nuage.
Mon zèle est fraîcheur du temps.

Mais l'abeille est songeuse
Et le gardon se couvre.
L'oiseau ne s'arrête pas.

II
CAPTIFS

Ma jeunesse en jouant fit la vie prisonnière.
Ô donjon où je vis!

Champs, vous vous mirez dans mes quatre moissons.
Je tonne, vous tournez.

FOURFOLD

I
SIDE BY SIDE

The meadows tell me of stream
And the streams of meadow.

The wind stays with the cloud.
My zeal is time's sharp air.

Yet the bee is pensive
And the fish is hiding in shadow.
The bird doesn't come to a halt.

II
CAPTIVES

My youth, playing, made life a captive.
O tower where I live!

Fields, you mirror yourselves in my four harvests.
I thunder, you turn.

III

L'OISEAU SPIRITUEL

Ne m'implorez pas, grands yeux; restez à couvert, désirs.
Je disparais au ciel, étangs privés de seuil.
Je glisse en liberté au travers des blés mûrs.
Nulle haleine ne teint le miroir de mon vol.
Je cours le malheur des humains, le dépulpe de son loisir.

IV

LIGNE DE FOI

La faveur des étoiles est de nous inviter à parler, de nous montrer que nous ne sommes pas seuls, que l'aurore a un toit et mon feu tes deux mains.

III

SPIRITUAL BIRD

Don't beg of me, large eyes; stay hidden, desires.
I vanish in the sky, ponds without thresholds.
I slip in freedom through the ripened wheat.
No breath blurs the mirror of my flight.
I roam through the human misfortune, squeeze the pulp of its leisure.

IV

LINE OF FAITH

The gift of the stars is to invite us to speak, to show us that we're not alone, that the dawn has a roof and my fire your two hands.

L'ISSUE

Tout s'éteignit:
Le jour, la lumière intérieure.
Masse endolorie,
Je ne trouvais plus mon temps vrai,
Ma maison.

L'amble des morts mal morts
Sonnant à tous les vides;
À un ciel nuageux
Je me délimitais.

Nourri par celui qui n'est pas du lieu,
Pas après pas, quasi consolé.

Pleine sera la vigne
Où combat ton épaule,
Sauf et même soleil.

OUTCOME

Everything was extinguished:
The day, the interior light.
An aching mass,
I could no longer find my true time,
My home.

The footfalls of those who have died cruel deaths
Sounding in all the voids;
To a clouded sky
I confined my scope.

Fed by the one who is not of the place,
Step after step, half-consoled.

The vine will be full,
Your shoulder will fight there,
Intact sunlight of old.

LE PAS OUVERT DE RENÉ CREVEL

Mais si les mots sont des bêches?

Alors la mort, en dessous, n'aura capté que ton écho.
Ta parole bouclée se confond toujours avec la vapeur exhalée par nos
    bouches
Quand l'hiver sème son givre sur nos manteaux.
L'esprit ne veut pas durcir comme pierre
Et lutte avec le limon qui l'entraîne à s'y essayer.
Mais le sommeil, le sommeil, est une bêche parcimonieuse.
Ô, qui veut partir, disparaisse dans la nuit que la douleur ne malmène plus!

THE BROAD STRIDE OF RENÉ CREVEL

But if words are spades?

Then death, below, will have captured only your echo.
Your completed word blends always with the vapor our mouths exhale
When winter sows its frost on our coats.
The mind hopes not to harden like a rock,
Fends off the silt that would draw it to such a state.
But sleep, sleep is a parsimonious spade.
Oh, he who wishes to depart, may he disappear in the night that pain no
    longer mars!

POUR UN PROMÉTHÉE SAXIFRAGE

En touchant la main éolienne de Hölderlin.

La réalité sans l'énergie disloquante de la poésie, qu'est-ce?

Dieu avait trop puissamment vécu parmi nous. Nous ne savions plus nous lever et partir. Les étoiles sont mortes dans nos yeux, qui furent souveraines dans son regard.

Ce sont les questions des anges qui ont provoqué l'irruption des démons. Ils nous fixèrent au rocher, pour nous battre et pour nous aimer. De nouveau.

La seule lutte a lieu dans les ténèbres. La victoire n'est que sur leurs bords.

Noble semence, guerre et faveur de mon prochain, devant la sourde aurore je te garde avec mon quignon, attendant ce jour prévu de haute pluie, de limon vert, qui viendra pour les brûlants, et pour les obstinés.

FOR A SAXIFRAGE PROMETHEUS

On touching the aeolian hand of Hölderlin.

Denise Naville

What's reality without the dislocating energy of poetry?

God had lived too powerfully among us. We no longer knew how to rise and depart. The stars that had been sovereign in his sight went dead in our eyes.

The questions of angels have provoked the irruption of demons. They fixed us to the rock, to lash us and to love us. Again.

The sole struggle takes place in the dark. There is victory only on its borders.

Noble seed, strife and friendship with my neighbor, before the muted dawn I hold you with my crust of bread, leaning toward the anticipated day of high rain, of rich silt, that will come for the passionate, and for the stubborn.

L'ESCALIER DE FLORE

Pourquoi vivant le plus vivant de tous, n'es-tu que ténèbres de fleur parmi les vivants?

Grège chaleur, lendemain tonnant, qui toucherez terre avant moi, ah! ne déposez pas ce qui bientôt sera masse d'amour pour vous.

THE STAIRS OF FLORA

Most fully living of all the living, why are you but a flower's dark among the living?

Raw heat that, with tomorrow's thunder, will touch the ground before me, ah! do not set down what will soon be a mass of love for you.

LA ROUTE PAR LES SENTIERS

Les sentiers, les entailles qui longent invisiblement la route, sont notre unique route, à nous qui parlons pour vivre, qui dormons, sans nous engourdir, sur le côté.

THE WAY OF THE SMALL PATHS

The footpaths, the cuts in earth invisibly running alongside the road, are the only road we take, we who speak to live, who sleep on our side and wake with a light step.

DÉCLARER SON NOM

J'avais dix ans. La Sorgue m'enchâssait. Le soleil chantait les heures sur le sage cadran des eaux. L'insouciance et la douleur avaient scellé le coq de fer sur le toit des maisons et se supportaient ensemble. Mais quelle roue dans le cœur de l'enfant aux aguets tournait plus fort, tournait plus vite que celle du moulin dans son incendie blanc?

TO STATE HIS NAME

I was ten years old. The Sorgue placed me in its shrine. The sun sang the hours on the waters' poised dial. Insouciance and pain, endured, enduring each other, had sealed the iron cock to the roofs of the houses. But what wheel in the heart of the watchful child turned more strongly, turned more rapidly, than the mill wheel in its white blaze?

TRAVERSE

La colline qu'il a bien servie descend en torrent dans son dos. Les langues pauvres le saluent; les mulets au pré lui font fête. La face rose de l'ornière tourne deux fois vers lui l'onde de son miroir. La méchanceté dort. Il est tel qu'il se rêvait.

SHORTCUT

The hill he has well served descends like a river at his back. Earthy tongues greet him; mules in the meadow welcome him. A rut in the trail, glinting, turns its undulant mirror toward him twice. Spitefulness has gone to sleep. He is as he dreamt himself.

SI . . .

Plus jamais nous ne serons rapatriés. Nous ne nous étirerons plus; nous ne mourrons plus dans un lointain fabuleux. Le ciel a pourri, jusqu'à son arc le plus distant; nul regard ne peut l'attiser. La terre est pareille à un ossement sans dévotion.

IF . . .

Never again will we make it back to our true country. We will no longer lean in space; we will no longer die in a distance found in words. The sky has rotted, even its farthest edge; no eye can revive it. The earth is like a bone no one prays for.

DE 1943

Tu as bien joui dans nos âmes,
Ô vieux sommeil de la putréfaction!

Depuis,
Lune après jour,
Vent après nuit,
Légers ou forts,
Nous attendons.

OF 1943

You've indeed feasted on our souls,
O ancient sleep of putrefaction.

Ever since,
Moon after day,
Wind after night,
Light or intense,
We wait.

LA FAUX RELEVÉE

Quand le bouvier des morts frappera du bâton,
Dédiez à l'été ma couleur dispersée.
Avec mes poings trop bleus étonnez un enfant.
Disposez sur ses joues ma lampe et mes épis.

Fontaine, qui tremblez dans votre étroit réduit,
Mon gain, aux soifs des champs, vous le prodiguerez.
De l'humide fougère au mimosa fiévreux,
Entre le vieil absent et le nouveau venu,
Le mouvement d'aimer, s'abaissant, vous dira:
«Hormis là, nul endroit, la disgrâce est partout.»

THE RAISED SCYTHE

When the herdsman of the dead strikes with his staff,
Dedicate to the summer my scattered color.
With my fists that are too blue astonish a child.
Lay on his cheeks my lamp and my ears of corn.

Fountain trembling in your austere redoubt,
You'll pour out what I've won to the thirsts of the fields.
From the humid fern to the feverish mimosa,
Between the old one gone and the new one come,
The pulse of love, descending, will say to you:
"Save for here, no place, disgrace is everywhere."

L'AVENIR NON PRÉDIT

Je te regarde vivre dans une fête que ma crainte de venir à fin laisse obscure.

Nos mains se ferment sur une étoile flagellaire. La flûte est à retailler.

À peine si la pointe d'un brutal soleil touche un jour débutant.

Ne sachant plus si tant de sève victorieuse devait chanter ou se taire, j'ai desserré le poing du Temps et saisi sa moisson.

Est apparu un multiple et stérile arc-en-ciel.

Ève solaire, possible de chair et de poussière, je ne crois pas au dévoilement des autres, mais au tien seul.

Qui gronde, me suive jusqu'à notre portail.

Je sens naître mon souffle nouveau et finir ma douleur.

THE FUTURE NOT FORETOLD

I watch you live in a celebration that my fear of coming to an end leaves darkened.

Our hands close upon a scourging star. The flute has to be recarved.

Barely does the angle of a brutal sun touch a day's beginning.

No longer knowing if so much victorious sap should sing or fall silent, I unclenched Time's fist and seized its harvest.

There appeared a multiple infertile rainbow.

Solar Eve, the possible of flesh and dust, I believe in the unveiling of none but you.

Let whoever thunders follow me to the gate.

I feel the birth of my new breath and the end of my pain.

ÉROS SUSPENDU

La nuit avait couvert la moitié de son parcours. L'amas des cieux allait à cette seconde tenir en entier dans mon regard. Je te vis, la première et la seule, divine femelle dans les sphères bouleversées. Je déchirai ta robe d'infini, te ramenai nue sur mon sol. L'humus mobile de la terre fut partout.

Nous volons, disent tes servantes, dans l'espace cruel,—au chant de ma trompette rouge.

EROS SUSPENDED

The night had covered half its route. At that moment the piled up skies were going to fit entirely in my gaze. I saw you, first and only, divine female in the upended spheres. I tore your robe of the infinite, brought you back naked to my ground. The loose clay of the earth was everywhere.

We fly, your servants say, in cruel space—to the song of my red trumpet.

NOUS TOMBONS

Ma brièveté est sans chaînes.

Baisers d'appui. Tes parcelles dispersées font soudain un corps sans regard.

Ô mon avalanche à rebours!

Toute liée.

Tel un souper dans le vent.

Toute liée. Rendue à l'air.

Tel un chemin rougi sur le roc. Un animal fuyant.

La profondeur de l'impatience et la verticale patience confondues.

La danse retournée. Le fouet belliqueux.

Tes limpides yeux agrandis.

Ces légers mots immortels jamais endeuillés.

Lierre à son rang silencieux.

Fronde que la mer approchait. Contre-taille du jour.

Abaisse encore ta pesanteur.

La mort nous bat du revers de sa fourche. Jusqu'à un matin sobre apparu en nous.

WE ARE FALLING

My brevity is without chains.

Kisses of support. Your scattered pieces suddenly form a body without a gaze.

O my avalanche in reverse!

Entirely connected.

Like a supper in the wind.

Entirely connected. Returned to air.

Like a path reddened on the rock. A fleeing animal.

The depth of impatience and vertical patience coming together.

The dance turned upside down. The bellicose whip.

Your limpid widened eyes.

These light immortal words never plunged in mourning.

Ivy in its silent row.

Catapult that the sea approached. Counter-thrust of the day.

Decrease your heaviness still further.

Death batters us with the back of its pitchfork. Until a sober morning appears in us.

LA MONTÉE DE LA NUIT

La fleur que je réchauffe, je double ses pétales, j'assombris sa corolle.

Le temps déchire et taille. Une lueur s'en éloigne: notre couteau.

Le printemps te capture et l'hiver t'émancipe, pays de bonds d'amour.

L'étoile me rend le dard de guêpe qui s'était enfoui en elle.

Veille, visage penché, tu irrigues le cœur des chèvres sur les pics.

THE ASCENT OF NIGHT

The flower that I warm, I double its petals, I darken its corolla.

Time rends and carves. A glimmer distances itself: our knife.

Spring captures you and winter frees you, country of love's elations.

The star gives me back the wasp's sting buried in it.

Stay awake, your head bent forward, you bring clear water to the hearts of the goats on the peaks.

QUITTER

DEPARTING

NOUS AVONS

Notre parole, en archipel, vous offre, après la douleur et le désastre, des fraises qu'elle rapporte des landes de la mort, ainsi que ses doigts chauds de les avoir cherchées.

Tyrannies sans delta, que midi jamais n'illumine, pour vous nous sommes le jour vieilli; mais vous ignorez que nous sommes aussi l'œil vorace, bien que voilé, de l'origine.

Faire un poème, c'est prendre possession d'un au-delà nuptial qui se trouve bien dans cette vie, très rattaché à elle, et cependant à proximité des urnes de la mort.

Il faut s'établir à l'extérieur de soi, au bord des larmes et dans l'orbite des famines, si nous voulons que quelque chose hors du commun se produise, qui n'était que pour nous.

Si l'angoisse qui nous évide abandonnait sa grotte glacée, si l'amante dans notre cœur arrêtait la pluie de fourmis, le Chant reprendrait.

Dans le chaos d'une avalanche, deux pierres s'épousant au bond purent s'aimer nues dans l'espace. L'eau de neige qui les engloutit s'étonna de leur mousse ardente.

L'homme fut sûrement le vœu le plus fou des ténèbres; c'est pourquoi nous sommes ténébreux, envieux et fous sous le puissant soleil.

Une terre qui était belle a commencé son agonie, sous le regard de ses sœurs voltigeantes, en présence de ses fils insensés.

*

Nous avons en nous d'immenses étendues que nous n'arriverons jamais à talonner; mais elles sont utiles à l'âpreté de nos climats, propices à notre éveil comme à nos perditions.

WE HAVE

Our word as archipelago gives you, after grief and disaster, strawberries it brings from the moors of death, and fingers warm from having gathered them.

Tyrannies without delta, which noon never illumines, for you we are the day grown old; but you are unaware that we are also the voracious eye, however veiled, of the origin.

To make a poem is to seize a nuptial beyond that's found well within this life, intimately connected to it, yet close to the urns of death.

We must build and dwell outside ourselves, on the edge of tears and in the orbit of famines, if we wish for something uncommon to take place, solely for us.

If the anguish that hollows us out were to abandon its frigid cave, if the lover in our hearts were to halt the rain of ants, the Song would revive.

In the chaos of an avalanche, two stones, married in the leap, came to love each other, naked in space. The snow-water that engulfed them was astonished by their ardent moss.

Man was surely the maddest vow of the dark; for this reason we are dark, fervent, and mad beneath the powerful sun.

An earth that was beautiful has entered its death throes, beneath the gaze of its fluttering sisters, in the presence of its insane sons.

*

We have within us immense expanses that we will never manage to cross; but they are helpful in the harshness of our climates, propitious to our awakening as well as our perditions.

Comment rejeter dans les ténèbres notre cœur antérieur et son droit de retour?

La poésie est ce fruit que nous serrons, mûri, avec liesse, dans notre main au même moment qu'il nous apparaît, d'avenir incertain, sur la tige givrée, dans le calice de la fleur.

Poésie, unique montée des hommes, que le soleil des morts ne peut assombrir dans l'infini parfait et burlesque.

*

Un mystère plus fort que leur malédiction innocentant leur cœur, ils plantèrent un arbre dans le Temps, s'endormirent au pied, et le Temps se fit aimant.

How can we cast out in the dark our earlier heart and its right of return?

Poetry is the ripe fruit that we hold in our hands, with joy, at the same moment as it appears, with an uncertain future, on the frost-covered stalk, in the flower's calyx.

Poetry, unique ascent of ours, that the sun of the dead cannot darken in the perfect and ludicrous infinite.

*

A mystery stronger than their curse making their hearts innocent again, they planted a tree in Time, went to sleep at its foot, and Time grew loving.

DANS LA MARCHE

Ces incessantes et phosphorescentes traînées de la mort sur soi que nous lisons dans les yeux de ceux qui nous aiment, sans désirer les leur dissimuler.

Faut-il distinguer entre une mort hideuse et une mort préparée de la main des génies? Entre une mort à visage de bête et une mort à visage de mort?

*

Nous ne pouvons vivre que dans l'entrouvert, exactement sur la ligne hermétique de partage de l'ombre et de la lumière. Mais nous sommes irrésistiblement jetés en avant. Toute notre personne prête aide et vertige à cette poussée.

La poésie est à la fois parole et provocation silencieuse, désespérée de notre être-exigeant pour la venue d'une réalité qui sera sans concurrente. Imputrescible celle-là. Impérissable, non; car elle court les dangers de tous. Mais la seule qui visiblement triomphe de la mort matérielle. Telle est la Beauté, la Beauté hauturière, apparue dès les premiers temps de notre cœur, tantôt dérisoirement conscient, tantôt lumineusement averti.

Ce qui gonfle ma sympathie, ce que j'aime, me cause bientôt presque autant de souffrance que ce dont je me détourne, en résistant, dans le mystère de mon cœur: apprêts voilés d'une larme.

La seule signature au bas de la vie blanche, c'est la poésie qui la dessine. Et toujours entre notre cœur éclaté et la cascade apparue.

Pour l'aurore, la disgrâce c'est le jour qui va venir; pour le crépuscule c'est la nuit qui engloutit. Il se trouva jadis des gens d'aurore. À cette heure de tombée, peut-être, nous voici. Mais pourquoi huppés comme des alouettes?

DURING THE JOURNEY

The incessant and phosphorescent flicker of death over our selves, which we read in the eyes of those who love us, without wishing to hide it from them.

Must we distinguish between a hideous death and a death prepared by the hands of geniuses? Between a death with the face of a beast and a death with the face of death?

*

We can only live in the half-opened, exactly on the hermetic boundary between the shadow and the light. But we are irresistibly thrown ahead. Our whole being lends support and vertigo to this push.

Poetry is at once word and the silent desperate provocation that we are, demanding the coming of a reality without rival. Incorruptible, this. Imperishable, no; for it meets with the same dangers as everyone. But it's the only reality that visibly prevails over material death. Such is Beauty, sea-roaming Beauty, which appears as far back as the first hours of our heart, now pathetically half-conscious, now luminously alert.

That which enlarges my sympathy, that which I love, soon causes me almost as much suffering as that which I turn away from, resist, in the mystery of my heart: preparations veiled with a tear.

It's poetry that traces the only signature at the base of the palpable light. And always between our heart that shatters and the waterfall that appears.

For dawn, misfortune is the day that's coming; for twilight, the night that swallows it. Once there were people of dawn to be found. At this hour of nightfall, perhaps, here we are. But why crested like larks?

L'ÉTERNITÉ À LOURMARIN

Albert Camus

Il n'y a plus de ligne droite ni de route éclairée avec un être qui nous a quittés. Où s'étourdit notre affection? Cerne après cerne, s'il approche c'est pour aussitôt s'enfouir. Son visage parfois vient s'appliquer contre le nôtre, ne produisant qu'un éclair glacé. Le jour qui allongeait le bonheur entre lui et nous n'est nulle part. Toutes les parties—presque excessives—d'une présence se sont d'un coup disloquées. Routine de notre vigilance . . . Pourtant cet être supprimé se tient dans quelque chose de rigide, de désert, d'essentiel en nous, où nos millénaires ensemble font juste l'épaisseur d'une paupière tirée.

Avec celui que nous aimons, nous avons cessé de parler, et ce n'est pas le silence. Qu'en est-il alors? Nous savons, ou croyons savoir. Mais seulement quand le passé qui signifie s'ouvre pour lui livrer passage. Le voici à notre hauteur, puis loin, devant.

À l'heure de nouveau contenue où nous questionnons tout le poids d'énigme, soudain commence la douleur, celle de compagnon à compagnon, que l'archer, cette fois, ne transperce pas.

ETERNITY AT LOURMARIN

Albert Camus

There is no longer a straight line or a clear road between ourselves and the one who has left us. Where is our affection dazed and made quiet? Ring after ring, if he approaches, no sooner does he bury himself. Sometimes his face comes to lean against ours, producing only a frozen glare. The day that extended happiness between him and us is nowhere. All the parts—almost excessive—of a presence are abruptly dislocated. The routine of our watchfulness . . . Yet this annulled being is held within something rigid, deserted, and essential in us, where all our millennia form the exact thickness of a shut eyelid.

With him whom we love, we have ceased to speak, and it is not silence. What is it? We know, or think we know. But only when the meaningful past opens to permit him passage. Here he is, in stride with us, then afar, in front.

In the hour again contained, when we question all the weight of enigma, suddenly the pain begins, pain reaching from one companion to another, which this time the archer doesn't pierce.

AUX RIVERAINS DE LA SORGUE

L'homme de l'espace dont c'est le jour natal sera un milliard de fois moins lumineux et révélera un milliard de fois moins de choses cachées que l'homme granité, reclus et recouché de Lascaux, au dur membre débourbé de la mort.

1959

TO THOSE WHO LIVE BY THE SORGUE

The man of outer space whose natal day this is will be a billion times less luminous, and reveal a billion times fewer hidden things, than the granite-like man of Lascaux, secluded, laid back to sleep, with his hard member cleared of the mud of death.

1959

CONTREVENIR

Obéissez à vos porcs qui existent. Je me soumets à mes dieux qui n'existent pas.

Nous restons gens d'inclémence.

COUNTERSTATEMENT

Obey your pigs that exist. I submit to my gods that do not exist.

We remain people of inclemency.

LES DENTELLES DE MONTMIRAIL

Au sommet du mont, parmi les cailloux, les trompettes de terre cuite des hommes des vieilles gelées blanches pépiaient comme de petits aigles.

Pour une douleur drue, s'il y a douleur.

La poésie vit d'insomnie perpétuelle.

Il semble que ce soit le ciel qui ait le dernier mot. Mais il le prononce à voix si basse que nul ne l'entend jamais.

Il n'y a pas de repli; seulement une patience millénaire sur laquelle nous sommes appuyés.

Dormez, désespérés, c'est bientôt jour, un jour d'hiver.

Nous n'avons qu'une ressource avec la mort: faire de l'art avant elle.

La réalité ne peut être franchie que soulevée.

Aux époques de détresse et d'improvisation, quelques-uns ne sont tués que pour une nuit et les autres pour l'éternité: un chant d'alouette des entrailles.

La quête d'un frère signifie presque toujours la recherche d'un être, notre égal, à qui nous désirons offrir des transcendances dont nous finissons à peine de dégauchir les signes.

Le probe tombeau: une meule de blé. Le grain au pain, la paille pour le fumier.

Ne regardez qu'une fois la vague jeter l'ancre dans la mer.

L'imaginaire n'est pas pur; il ne fait qu'aller.

Les grands ne se perpétuent que par les grands. On oublie. La mesure seule est blessée.

THE DENTELLES DE MONTMIRAIL

At the mountain's summit, among the stones, the clay trumpets of men of ancient hoarfrost were crying like small eagles.

If there be sorrow, let it be dense sorrow.

Poetry is sustained by perpetual insomnia.

It seems it is the sky that has the last word. But it speaks in a voice so low that no one hears it.

There is no place of withdrawal; only a millennial patience we stand on.

Sleep, desperate ones, it will soon be day, a winter day.

We have only one recourse with death: to precede it in the making of art.

Reality can be surpassed only by being provoked.

In epochs of distress and improvisation, some are killed only for a night, others for eternity: a lark's song in the depths.

The quest for a brother almost always means the search for a being, our equal, to whom we want to offer transcendences of which we have barely finished carving the signs.

The honest tomb: a wheat stack. Grain for bread, straw for dung.

Only once watch the wave drop the anchor in the sea.

The space of imagination is not pure; it simply goes.

Great souls are perpetuated only by great souls. We forget. The measure alone is harmed.

Qu'est-ce qu'un nageur qui ne saurait se glisser entièrement sous les eaux?

Avec des poings pour frapper, ils firent de pauvres mains pour travailler.

Les pluies sauvages favorisent les passants profonds.

L'essentiel est ce qui nous escorte, en temps voulu, en allongeant la route. C'est aussi une lampe sans regard, dans la fumée.

L'écriture d'un bleu fanal, pressée, dentelée, intrépide, du Ventoux alors enfant, courait toujours sur l'horizon de Montmirail qu'à tout moment notre amour m'apportait, m'enlevait.

Des débris de rois d'une inexpugnable férocité.

Les nuages ont des desseins aussi fermés que ceux des hommes.

Ce n'est pas l'estomac qui réclame la soupe bien chaude, c'est le cœur.

Sommeil sur la plaie pareil à du sel.

Une ingérence innommable a ôté aux choses, aux circonstances, aux êtres, leur hasard d'auréole. Il n'y a d'avènement pour nous qu'à partir de cette auréole. Elle n'immunise pas.

Cette neige, nous l'aimions, elle n'avait pas de chemin, elle découvrait notre faim.

What's a swimmer incapable of gliding entirely underwater?

With fists for striking, they made poor hands for working.

Thundering rains favor the deeper passersby.

The essential is what escorts us, in due time, by extending the road. It's also a lamp without an eye, in the smoke.

The urgent, jagged, bold writing of a blue lantern—of Ventoux in its childhood—always ran on the horizon of Montmirail that at every moment our love brought me, took away from me.

The remains of kings of inexpugnable ferocity.

Clouds have designs as inscrutable as ours.

It's not the stomach that begs for the hot soup, it's the heart.

A sleep on the wound akin to salt.

An unspeakable meddling has taken from things, from circumstances, from lives, their brightening chance. There is no advent for us other than from this brightening. It does not bring invulnerability.

That snow, we loved it, it had no tracks, it uncovered our hunger.

L'ALLÉGRESSE

Les nuages sont dans les rivières, les torrents parcourent le ciel. Sans saisie les journées montent en graine, meurent en herbe. Le temps de la famine et celui de la moisson, l'un sous l'autre dans l'air haillonneux, ont effacé leur différence. Ils filent ensemble, ils bivaquent! Comment la peur serait-elle distincte de l'espoir, passant raviné? Il n'y a plus de seuil aux maisons, de fumée aux clairières. Est tombé au gouffre le désir de chaleur—et ce peu d'obscurité dans notre dos où s'inquiétait la primevère dès qu'épiait l'avenir.

Pont sur la route des invasions, mentant au vainqueur, exorable au défait. Saurons-nous, sous le pied de la mort, si le cœur, ce gerbeur, ne doit pas précéder mais suivre?

ELATION

Clouds are in the rivers, torrents cross the sky. Uncaptured, the days go to seed, die unripe. The time of famine and the time of harvest, one beneath the other in the tattered air, have erased their difference. They pass by swiftly together, they camp together! How could fear be distinct from hope, furrowed passerby? Gone are the thresholds in the houses now, gone is the smoke in the clearings. Into the abyss has fallen the desire for heat—and that bit of darkness at our back where the primrose would worry as soon as it took to watching for the future.

Bridge on the road of invasions, deceptive to the victor, merciful to the defeated. Will we know, under the foot of death, if the heart, this binder of sheaves, should not precede but follow?

FONTIS

Le raisin a pour patrie
Les doigts de la vendangeuse.
Mais elle, qui a-t-elle,
Passé l'étroit sentier de la vigne cruelle?

Le rosaire de la grappe;
Au soir le très haut fruit couchant qui saigne
La dernière étincelle.

WHERE THE EARTH GIVES WAY

The grapes have for their native country
The fingers of the woman harvesting them.
But she, whom does she have,
The thin path of the cruel vine behind her?

The rosary of grapes;
At dusk, above, the setting fruit that bleeds
The last gleam.

DEDICATIONS

Le Rempart de brindilles is dedicated to Yves Battistini.

Le Mortel Partenaire is dedicated to Maurice Blanchot.

Le Risque et le Pendule is dedicated to René Ménard.

Les Compagnons dans le jardin is dedicated to André du Bouchet and Jacques Dupin.

Dans la marche is dedicated to Georges Blin.

L'Éternité à Lourmarin is dedicated to Jean-Paul Samson.

NOTES

p. 45   "From the white Lady of Africa / To the Magdalen beside the mirror"
While the expression "the white Lady of Africa" is not entirely clear,
in the context it is plausible to read it as a reference to a prehistoric
cave painting in the Brandberg Mountains of Namibia. The abbé Henri
Breuil reproduces and briefly discusses this painting in the opening pages
of his *Quatres cents siècles d'art pariétal* (Paris: Montignac, 1952), where
he calls the painted figure "la dame blanche d'Afrique." Contemporary
scholars tend to dismiss Breuil's account of this painting. Yet his book
was an early and influential study of prehistoric cave art throughout
Italy, Spain, and France. Lascaux was discovered in 1940 by three boys
playing in the hills of Montignac.

Throughout Char's poetry there are allusions, and at times explicit
references, to paintings by Georges de La Tour (1593–1652). The
"Magdalen beside the mirror" in this poem appears to allude to a famous
painting by La Tour known in English as *The Penitent Magdalen*. In this
painting the Magdalen is seated to the side of a table on which a mirror
and a candle are set, the mirror reflecting not her but the lighted candle;
her hands are folded on top of a skull, a memento mori, which rests on
her lap.

p. 53   *La Minutieuse*
The title is not translatable. The adjective *minutieuse* means "meticulous,"
"demandingly precise," and "marked by a keen attention to detail, to
minutiae." In this poem the adjective has become a noun and, further,
the name of a feminine companion or presence.

p. 75   Dabo
Char served in the French army from September 1939, when Germany
invaded Poland, and France and England declared war on Germany,
through June 1940, when France surrendered. During this period Char
was stationed in Alsace, through which the Vosges mountain range runs.
Dabo is a small village in the neighboring region of Lorraine, located
about thirty miles west of Strasbourg.

p. 77   La Petite-Pierre d'Alsace

La Petite-Pierre d'Alsace is a small village in Alsace.

p. 87   Response to a painter

According to Greilsamer (286-89), the poem is addressed to Nicolas de Staël (1914–55). Staël and Char became friends in the years after the war. In the late summer and fall of 1953, Staël, his family, and two friends to whom Char had introduced him, Ciska Grillet and Jeanne Mathieu, traveled to Sicily, where they spent time in Agrigento, a city founded by Greek colonists in the sixth century BCE. The landscape of southern Sicily made a deep impression on Staël.

p. 135   Mourning for Névons

Les Névons was the name of the Char family home in L'Isle-sur-la-Sorgue. The large park surrounding the house was sold in 1955. When Char's older brother put the park up for auction, Char and his older sister, Émilienne, had hoped to buy it, but they lacked the funds to do so (Greilsamer, 293-96).

p. 189   Lourmarin

Lourmarin is a small village in the Vaucluse region of Provence. Camus (1913-60) bought a house there a short time before his death.

    Camus and Char met after the war and became close friends in the fifties. Camus cited Char appreciatively in the last chapter of his controversial work *L'Homme révolté*. He also wrote a short essay on Char, "René Char," an English translation of which can be found in his *Lyrical and Critical Essays* (New York: Knopf, 1968). Char's short prose appreciation of Camus, "Je veux parler d'un ami" ("I want to speak of a friend"), included in his *Recherche de la base et du sommet*, has not, to my knowledge, been translated into English.

p. 195   The Dentelles de Montmirail

The Dentelles de Montmirail is a small mountain range in the Vaucluse, named for its "lace-like" or jagged appearance. Rising above these mountains is Mont Ventoux.

ACKNOWLEDGMENTS

I began this translation in great solitude and it became by far the most collaborative work I've ever done. There are many people I would like to thank here. For a long time I've read and on occasion taught the books of Char's previous translators, in particular those of Jackson Mathews, Cid Corman, Mary Ann Caws, and Nancy Kline, translators who have surely had an influence on the way I understand Char's poetry. Melissa Kwasny was a deeply attentive reader of these poems at every station of the journey. Rusty Morrison and Ken Keegan, my editors, have been marvelously clear and supportive. I'm especially grateful to them for their patience. Lise Lalonde, a former student of mine, helped me with these poems in all sorts of ways. Jonathan Culler, Sarah Gridley, and Kevin Hart shared with me their thoughts about particular poems and about the path of translation. I owe a particularly large debt to two people who engaged the entire book in detail. Rose Vekony responded to an earlier draft of the translation with a great many clarifying suggestions. Ann Smock gave an earlier draft of the translation an invaluable critical reading, bringing to the poems her knowledge of French poetry, her experience in translation, and a generously demanding attention. Whatever weaknesses remain in the translation are of course my responsibility. That said, many of the strengths in the translation have come, directly or indirectly, from the readers I've named here. My deepest thanks to these readers for all the time and care they have given to this book.

René Char is one of the great French poets of the last century. He was born in L'Isle-sur-la-Sorgue, in 1907, and lived almost all his life in either Paris or Provence. As a young writer, he participated in the surrealist movement, but in 1935 he broke with the movement and began to find his own path. He fought in the Second World War and in its darkest years became a leader in the Resistance. His many books of poetry, including a wartime notebook published in 1946, *Leaves of Hypnos*, earned him recognition as one of the major existential writers of his time, a poet of passion and independence, presence of mind and speculative scope. He died in 1988.

*

Robert Baker studied at the Univerity of Wisconsin in Madison, the Universidad Complutense de Madrid, and Cornell University, where he received a PhD in Comparative Literature. The author of two books, *The Extravagant: Crossings of Modern Poetry and Modern Philosophy* and *In Dark Again in Wonder: The Poetry of René Char and George Oppen*, he is professor of English at the University of Montana.

The Word as Archipelago
by René Char
Translated by Robert Baker

Cover text set in Trajan Pro and Cochin LT Std.
Interior text set in Adobe Garamond Pro.

Cover art: Lascaux Cave, frieze of swimming stags.
(Photo N. Aujoulat-CNP-MCC.)

Cover and interior design by Cassandra Smith

Omnidawn Publishing
Richmond, California
2012

Ken Keegan & Rusty Morrison, Co-Publishers & Senior Editors
Cassandra Smith, Poetry Editor & Book Designer
Gillian Hamel, Poetry Editor & OmniVerse Managing Editor
Sara Mumolo, Poetry Editor & OmniVerse New-Work Editor
Peter Burghardt, Poetry Editor & Bookstore Outreach Manager
Turner Canty, Poetry Editor & Features Writer
Jared Alford, Facebook Editor
Juliana Paslay, Bookstore Outreach & Features Writer
Craig Santos Perez, Media Consultant